Best Easy Day Hikes
Absaroka-Beartooth Wilderness

Help Us Keep This Guide Up to Date

Every effort has been made by the author and editors to make this guide as accurate and useful as possible; however, many things can change after a guide is published—regulations change, facilities come under new management, and so forth.

We would love to hear from you concerning your experiences with this guide and how you feel it could be improved and kept up to date. While we may not be able to respond to all comments and suggestions, we'll take them to heart, and we'll also make certain to share them with the author. Please send your comments and suggestions to falconeditorial@rowman.com.

Thanks for your input!

Best Easy Day Hikes Series

Best Easy Day Hikes
Absaroka-Beartooth
Wilderness

Fourth Edition

Bill Schneider

FALCONGUIDES

ESSEX, CONNECTICUT

FALCONGUIDES®

An imprint of Globe Pequot, the trade division of
The Rowman & Littlefield Publishing Group, Inc.
4501 Forbes Blvd., Ste. 200
Lanham, MD 20706
www.rowman.com

Distributed by NATIONAL BOOK NETWORK

British Library Cataloguing in Publication Information available

Library of Congress Cataloging-in-Publication Data Available

ISBN 978-1-4930-7239-2 (paperback)
ISBN 978-1-4930-7240-8 (e-book)

Contents

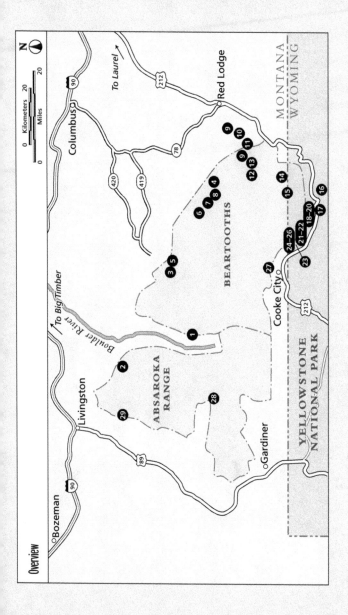

Overview

Introduction

What Is a "Best Easy" Day Hike?

One of the beauties of hiking is that there are hikes for virtually anyone, whether beginner or experienced, overnight backpacker or day-tripper. Of all the hiking I've done over the past fifty years, the hikes in this book are my favorite easy day hikes in the Absaroka-Beartooth Wilderness.

Best Easy Day Hikes Absaroka-Beartooth Wilderness is a companion volume to my more comprehensive guidebook *Hiking the Absaroka-Beartooth Wilderness*, which covers every trail in the Beartooths and most in the Absaroka Range, including quite a few that are neither "best" nor "easy." *Best East Day Hikes Absaroka-Beartooth Wilderness* includes only short, modestly strenuous hikes that are my recommendations for the nicest easy day hikes in this magnificent wilderness.

These hikes vary in length—most are short, and a few are moderate in length. With a few exceptions, none have seriously big hills, and those that do have a steep upgrade are short. In other words, there are no long hikes with big hills. All hikes are on easy-to-follow trails, and with one exception (Hellroaring Plateau, Hike 14), there are no off-trail sections.

Some of the hikes in this book may seem challenging to some hikers but easy to others. To help you select the right hike, I've ranked the hikes from easiest to hardest. Please keep in mind that short does not always equal easy. Other factors, such as elevation gain and trail conditions, have to be considered.

I hope you thoroughly enjoy your "best easy" hiking in one of America's finest hiking areas.

—Bill Schneider

Two Wildernesses in One

The magnificent Absaroka-Beartooth Wilderness is split into two distinctly different regions. The Beartooths get most of the fame and attract legions of hikers. Locally called the Beartooth Plateau, this high-altitude, lake-strewn uplift has a wonderful system of well-traveled trails, some starting at high elevation along the scenic Beartooth Highway. The Absaroka Range is a more typical western mountain range that doesn't have as good a trail system but still offers some terrific hiking—though not as many Best Easy Day Hikes.

A Short Season for Hiking

More than most hiking areas, the Beartooth Plateau has a short hiking season. The high-elevation area usually remains covered with snow into July, and even in July, there is so much water and so many lingering snowbanks, hikers can plan on having soaked feet most of the day. The "prime time" to go hiking here is from late July through early September. The Absaroka Range has a slightly longer hiking season: early July through September.

Watch the Weather

The Absaroka Range and the Beartooths are widely known for unpredictable weather, and this usually means bad weather. It can snow any day of the year in these mountains. Even while on short day hikes, carefully watch the weather, and always be prepared with warm clothing and raingear.

Mosquito Haven

If the conditions are just right (wrong?), the Absaroka-Beartooth can almost disappear under the clouds of mosquitoes, so be prepared with bug dope and mosquito netting. Early frosts sometimes knock down the mosquito population, so hiking later in the season (mid August and early September) might mean fewer bugs.

How to Use This Guide

Types of Hikes

Three types of hikes are described in this book:

Loop: You start and finish at the same trailhead, with no (or very little) retracing of your steps.

Shuttle: This point-to-point trip requires two vehicles (one left at the other end of the trail) or a prearranged pickup at a designated time and place.

Out-and-back: You travel to a specific destination, then retrace your steps back to the trailhead.

Map Sense

The Absaroka-Beartooth Wilderness has several options for maps, and good maps are essential to any wilderness trip. Maps help you find routes and "stay found." Plus, many hikers would not want to miss out on the unending joy of mindlessly whittling away untold hours staring at a map and wondering what the world looks like here and there.

For trips into the Absaroka-Beartooth, there are at least three excellent maps covering the entire wilderness:

- *The Forest Service Absaroka-Beartooth Wilderness* map, which is currently somewhat outdated, but a new version is in the works. Until the new map comes out, a good alternative is the Gallatin National Forest Central map, which will also soon be replaced by a new map covering the recently combined Custer Gallatin National Forest.

- *The Absaroka-Beartooth Wilderness* map published by Beartooth Publishing of Bozeman, Montana.
- The *Trails Illustrated/National Geographic Maps* (East and West) covering the entire wilderness.

For more detailed maps covering parts of the wilderness, usually in larger scale and with more detail:

- US Geological Survey (USGS) topographic maps.
- A series of six topo maps published by Rocky Mountain Survey (RMS), a private company in Billings, Montana, designed especially for serious hikers and anglers.
- Ranger district maps published by the Forest Service.

The Vehicle You Need to Reach the Trailheads

Usually this isn't a huge problem, but in the Absaroka-Beartooth, it can be, especially to access the Hellroaring Plateau trailhead, which almost requires an ATV to reach, but at the minimum a four-wheel-drive, high-clearance vehicle with low-range gearing and the four-wheeling expertise to go with it. Other trailheads have bumpy, dusty roads but are accessible with any vehicle: Glacier Lake, West Rosebud, East Rosebud, and all the trailheads in the West Fork of Rock Creek. To reach the West Stillwater Trailhead, you'd feel more comfortable with a 4WD, but with care, you can make it with any vehicle. The rest of the trailheads are on paved roads.

For More Information

The Forest Service is the best source of information on the Absaroka-Beartooth Wilderness. Unfortunately, with four ranger districts managing parts of this wilderness, the exact areas of management can be confusing. Also, some trails go from one ranger district to another. The best approach is to contact the ranger district closest to the trailhead you intend to use.

Call or write the ranger districts at the following addresses:

Custer Gallatin National Forest
Beartooth Ranger District
6811 Highway 212
Red Lodge, MT 59068
(406) 446-2103

Custer Gallatin National Forest
Gardiner Ranger District
805 Scott St.
Gardiner, MT 59030
(406) 848-7375

Custer Gallatin National Forest
Yellowstone Ranger District
5242 Highway 89 South
Livingston, MT 59047
(406) 222-1892

Shoshone National Forest
Clarks Fork, Greybull,
Wapiti Ranger District
203A Yellowstone Ave.
Cody, WY 82414
(307) 527-6241

Zero Impact

Going into a wilderness area is like visiting a famous museum. You obviously do not want to leave your mark on an art treasure in the museum. If everybody going through the museum left one little mark, the piece of art would quickly be destroyed—and of what value is a big building full of trashed art? The same goes for a pristine wilderness such as the Absaroka-Beartooth, which is as magnificent as any masterpiece by any artist. If we all left just one little mark on the landscape, the wilderness would soon be despoiled.

A wilderness can accommodate human use as long as everybody behaves. But a few thoughtless or uninformed visitors can ruin it for everybody who follows. All wilderness users have a responsibility to know and follow the rules of zero-impact hiking and camping. An important source of these guidelines, including the most updated research, can be found in the book *Leave No Trace*.

Nowadays most wilderness users want to walk softly, but some aren't aware that they have poor manners. Often their actions are dictated by the outdated habits of a past generation of campers who cut green boughs for evening shelters, built campfires with fire rings, and dug trenches around tents. In the 1950s these "camping rules" may have been acceptable. But they leave long-lasting scars, and today such behavior is absolutely unacceptable. The wilderness is shrinking, and the number of users is mushrooming. More and more camping areas show unsightly signs of heavy use.

Consequently, a new code of ethics is growing out of the necessity of coping with the unending waves of people who want a perfect wilderness experience. Today, we all must leave no clues that we have gone before. Canoeists can look behind the canoe and see no trace of their passing. Hikers, mountain bikers, and four-wheelers should have the same goal. Enjoy the wilderness, but leave no trace of your visit.

Three Zero-Impact Principles

- Leave with everything you brought in.
- Leave no sign of your visit.
- Leave the landscape as you found it.

Most of us know better than to litter in or out of the wilderness. Be sure you leave nothing, regardless of how small it is, along the trail or at the campsite. This means you should pack out everything, including orange peels, flip tops, cigarette butts, and gum wrappers. Also, pick up any trash that others leave behind.

Follow the main trail. Avoid cutting switchbacks and walking on vegetation beside the trail.

Don't pick up "souvenirs," such as rocks, antlers, or wildflowers. The next person wants to see them, too.

Avoid making loud noises that may disturb others. Remember, sound travels easily to the other side of the lake. Be courteous.

Carry a lightweight trowel to bury human waste 6 to 8 inches deep, and pack out used toilet paper. Keep human waste at least 300 feet from any water source.

Finally, and perhaps most importantly, strictly follow the pack-in/pack-out rule. If you carry something into the backcountry, consume it or carry it out.

Make zero impact—and put your ear to the ground in the wilderness and listen carefully. Thousands of people coming behind you are thanking you for your courtesy and good sense.

Have a Safe Trip

Scouts have been guided for decades by what is perhaps the best single piece of safety advice: Be prepared! For starters, this means carrying survival and first-aid materials, proper clothing, compass, and topographic map—and knowing how to use them.

Perhaps the second-best piece of safety advice is to tell somebody where you're going and when you plan to return.

Pilots file flight plans before every trip, and anybody venturing into a blank spot on the map should do the same. File your "flight plan" with a friend or relative before taking off.

Close behind your flight plan and being prepared with proper equipment is physical conditioning. Being fit not only makes wilderness travel more fun, it makes it safer. To whet your appetite for more knowledge of wilderness safety and preparedness, here are a few more tips.

- Check the weather forecast. Be careful not to get caught at high altitude by a bad storm or along a stream in a flash flood. Watch cloud formations closely, so you don't get stranded on a ridgeline during a lightning storm. Avoid traveling during prolonged periods of cold weather.
- Avoid traveling alone in the wilderness.
- Keep your party together.
- Study basic survival and first aid before leaving home.
- Don't eat wild plants unless you have positively identified them and know they are safe to eat.
- Before you leave for the trailhead, find out as much as you can about the route, especially the potential hazards.
- Don't exhaust yourself or other members of your party by traveling too far or too fast. Let the slowest person set the pace.
- Don't wait until you're confused to look at your maps. Follow them as you go along from the moment you start moving up the trail, so you have a continual fix on your location.
- If you get lost, don't panic. Sit down and relax for a few minutes while you carefully check your topo map and take a reading with your compass. Confidently plan your

next move. It's often smart to retrace your steps until you find familiar ground, even if you think it might lengthen your trip. Lots of people get temporarily lost in the wilderness and survive usually by calmly and rationally dealing with the situation.

- Stay clear of all wild animals.
- Take a first-aid kit that includes, at a minimum, the following items: sewing needle, snakebite kit, aspirin, antibacterial ointment, two antiseptic swabs, two butterfly bandages, adhesive tape, four adhesive strips, four gauze pads, two triangular bandages, codeine tablets, two inflatable splints, moleskin or Second Skin for blisters, one roll 3-inch gauze, CPR shield, rubber gloves, and lightweight first-aid instructions.
- Take a survival kit that includes, at a minimum, the following items: compass, whistle, matches in a waterproof container, cigarette lighter, candle, signal mirror, flashlight, fire starter, aluminum foil, water-purification tablets, space blanket, and flare.

Last but not least, don't forget that the best defense against unexpected hazards is knowledge. Read up on the latest in wilderness safety information.

You Might Never Know What Hit You

The high-altitude topography of the Absaroka-Beartooth Wilderness is prone to sudden thunderstorms, especially in July and August. If you get caught in a lightning storm, take special precautions. Remember:

- Lightning can travel far ahead of the storm, so be sure to take cover before the storm hits.

- Don't try to make it back to your vehicle. It isn't worth the risk. Instead, seek shelter even if it's only a short way back to the trailhead. Lightning storms usually don't last long, and from a safe vantage point, you might enjoy the sights and sounds.

- Be especially careful not to get caught on a mountaintop or exposed ridge, under large solitary trees, in the open, or near standing water.

- Seek shelter in a low-lying area, ideally in a dense stand of small, uniformly sized trees.

- Stay away from anything that might attract lightning, such as metal tent poles, graphite fishing rods, or pack frames.

- Get in a crouch position and place both feet firmly on the ground.

- If you have a pack (without a metal frame) or a sleeping pad with you, put your feet on it for extra insulation against shock.

- Don't walk or huddle together with others. Instead, stay 50 feet or more from one another, so if somebody gets hit by lightning, others in your party can give first aid.

- If you're in a tent, stay there, in your sleeping bag with your feet on your sleeping pad.

The Silent Killer

Be aware of the danger of hypothermia—a condition in which the body's internal temperature drops below normal. It can lead to mental and physical collapse and death. This is a special item of concern when hiking in the Absaroka-Beartooth, particularly on the Beartooth Plateau, where you can get nailed with 6 inches of snow any day of the year.

Hypothermia is caused by exposure to cold and is aggravated by wetness, wind, and exhaustion. The moment you begin to lose heat faster than your body produces it, you're suffering from exposure. Your body starts involuntary exercise, such as shivering to stay warm, and makes involuntary adjustments to preserve normal temperature in vital organs, restricting blood flow in the extremities. Both responses drain your energy reserves. The only way to stop the drain is to reduce the degree of exposure.

With full-blown hypothermia, as energy reserves are exhausted, cold reaches the brain, depriving you of good judgment and reasoning power. You won't be aware that this is happening. You lose control of your hands. Your internal temperature slides downward. Without treatment, this slide leads to stupor, collapse, and death.

To defend against hypothermia, stay dry. When clothes get wet, they lose most of their insulating value. High-tech synthetics are your best choice for retaining heat and repelling moisture. Choose rain clothes that cover the head, neck, body, and legs and provide good protection against wind-driven rain. Most hypothermia cases develop in air temperatures between 30°F and 50°F, but hypothermia can develop in warmer temperatures.

If your party is exposed to wind, cold, and wet, think hypothermia. Watch yourself and others for these symptoms: uncontrollable fits of shivering; vague, slow, slurred speech; memory lapses; incoherence; immobile, fumbling hands; frequent stumbling or a lurching gait; drowsiness (to sleep is to die); apparent exhaustion; and inability to get up after a rest. When a member of your party has hypothermia, he or she may deny any problem. Believe the symptoms, not the victim. Even mild symptoms demand treatment, as follows:

- Get the victim out of the wind and rain.
- Strip off all wet clothes.
- If the victim is only mildly impaired, give them warm drinks. Then get the victim into warm clothes and a warm sleeping bag. Place well-wrapped water bottles filled with heated water close to the victim.

If the victim is badly impaired, attempt to keep them awake. Put the victim in a sleeping bag with another person—both naked (not a time for modesty). If you have a double bag, put two warm people in with the victim.

Be Bear Aware

The first step of any hike in bear country is an attitude adjustment. Nothing guarantees total safety. Hiking in bear country adds a small additional risk to your trip. However, that risk can be greatly minimized by adhering to this age-old piece of advice: Be prepared. And being prepared doesn't only mean having the right equipment. It also means having the right information. Knowledge is your best defense.

You can—and should—thoroughly enjoy your trip to bear country. Don't let the fear of bears ruin your vacation. This fear can accompany you every step of the way. It can be constantly lurking in the back of your mind, preventing you from enjoying the wildest and most beautiful places left on Earth. And even worse, some bear experts think bears might actually be able to sense your fear.

Being prepared and knowledgeable gives you confidence. It allows you to fight back the fear that can burden you throughout your stay in bear country. You won't—nor should you—forget about bears and the basic rules of safety, but proper preparation allows you to keep the fear of bears at bay and let enjoyment rule the day.

And on top of that, do we really want to be totally safe? If we did, we probably would never go hiking in the wilderness—bears or no bears. We certainly wouldn't, at much greater risk, drive hundreds of miles to get to the trailhead. Perhaps a tinge of danger adds a desired element to our wilderness trip.

Day Hiking in Bear Country

Nobody likes surprises, and bears dislike them, too. The majority of bear maulings occur when a hiker surprises a bear. Therefore, it's vital to do everything possible to avoid these surprise meetings. Perhaps the best way is to know this five-part system. If you adhere to the following five rules, the chance of encountering a bear on the trail sinks to the slimmest possible margin.

- Be alert.
- Go with a group and stay together.
- Stay on the trail.
- Hike in the middle of the day.
- Make noise.

There's no substitute for alertness: As you hike, watch ahead and to the sides. Don't fall into the all-too-common and particularly nasty habit of fixating on the trail 10 feet ahead. It's especially easy to do this when dragging a heavy pack up a long hill or when carefully watching your step on a heavily eroded trail.

Using your knowledge of bear habitats and habits, be especially alert in areas most likely to be frequented by bears such as avalanche chutes, berry patches, streams, stands of whitebark pine, and so forth.

Watch carefully for bear signs, and be especially watchful (and noisy) if you see any. If you see a track or a scat, but it doesn't look fresh, pretend it's fresh. This area is obviously frequented by bears.

Watch the wind: The wind can be a friend or foe. The strength and direction of the wind can make a significant difference in your chances of an encounter with a bear. When the wind is blowing at your back, your smell travels ahead of you, alerting any bear that might be on or near the trail ahead. Conversely, when the wind blows in your face, your chances of a surprise meeting with a bear increase, so make more noise and be more alert.

A strong wind can also be noisy and limit a bear's ability to hear you coming. If a bear can't smell or hear you coming, the chances of an encounter greatly increase, so watch the wind.

Safety in numbers: There have been very few instances where a large group has had an encounter with a bear. On the other hand, a large percentage of hikers mauled by bears were hiking alone. Large groups naturally make more noise and put out more smell and probably appear more threatening to bears. In addition, if you're hiking alone and get injured, there is nobody to go for help. For these reasons, rangers often recommend parties of four or more hikers when going into bear country.

If the large party splits up, the advantage is lost, so stay together. If you're on a family hike, keep the kids from running ahead. If you're in a large group, keep the stronger members from going ahead or weaker members from lagging behind. The best way to prevent this natural separation is to ask one of the slowest members of the group to lead. This keeps everybody together.

Stay on the trail: Although bears use trails, they don't often use them during midday hours, when hikers commonly use them. Through generations of associating trails with people, bears probably expect to find hikers on trails, especially during midday.

Contrarily, bears probably don't expect to find hikers off trails. Bears rarely settle down in a daybed right along a heavily used trail. However, if you wander around in thickets off the trail, you are more likely to stumble into an occupied daybed or cross paths with a traveling bear.

Sleeping late: Bears—and most other wildlife—usually aren't active during the middle of a day, especially on a hot summer day. Wild animals are most active around dawn and dusk. Therefore, hiking early in the morning or late afternoon increases your chances of seeing wildlife, including bears. Likewise, hiking during midday on a hot August day greatly reduces the chance of an encounter.

Sounds: Perhaps the best way to avoid a surprise meeting with a bear is to make sure the bear knows you're coming, so make lots of noise. Some experts think metallic noise is superior to human voices, which can be muffled by natural conditions, but the important issue is making lots of noise, regardless of what kind of noise.

Running: Many avid runners like to get off paved roads and running tracks and onto backcountry trails. But running on trails in bear country can be seriously hazardous to your health. Bears can't hear you coming and you approach them faster than expected, and of course, it's nearly impossible to keep alert while running when you have to watch the trail closely to keep from falling.

Leave the night to the bears: Like running on trails, hiking at night can be very risky. Bears are more active after dark, and you can't see them until it's too late. If you get caught at night, be sure to make lots of noise, and remember that bears commonly travel on hiking trails at night.

You can be dead meat, too: If you see or smell a carcass of a dead animal when hiking, immediately vacate the area. Don't let your curiosity keep you near the carcass a second longer than necessary. Bears commonly hang around a carcass, guarding it and feeding on it for days until it's completely consumed. Your presence could easily be interpreted as a threat to the bear's food supply, and a vicious attack could be imminent.

If you see a carcass ahead of you on the trail, don't go any closer. Instead, abandon your hike and return to the trailhead. If the carcass is between you and the trailhead, take a very long detour around it, upwind from the carcass, making lots of noise along the way. Be sure to report the carcass to the local ranger. This might prompt a temporary trail closure or special warnings and prevent injury to other hikers. Rangers will, in some cases, go in and drag the carcass away from the trail.

Cute, cuddly, and lethal: If you see a bear cub, don't go one inch closer to it. It might seem abandoned, but it most likely is not. Mother bear is probably very close, and female bears fiercely defend their young.

Bear repellent doesn't do you any good in your pack: If you brought a repellent such as pepper spray, don't bury it in your pack. Keep it as accessible as possible. Most pepper spray comes in a holster or somehow conveniently attaches to your belt or pack. Such protection won't do you any good if you can't have it ready to fire in one or two seconds. Before hitting the trail, read the directions carefully and test-fire the spray.

Regulations: Nobody likes rules and regulations. However, national parks have a few that you must follow. These rules aren't meant to take the freedom out of your trip. They are meant to help bring you back safely.

But I didn't see any bears: Now, you know how to be safe. Walk up the trail constantly clanging two metal pans together. It works every time. You won't see a bear, but you'll hate your "wilderness experience." You left the city to get away from loud noise.

Yes, you can be very safe, but how safe do you want to be and still be able to enjoy your trip? It's a balancing act. First,

The "Bear" Essentials of Day Hiking in Bear Country

- Knowledge is the best defense.
- There is no substitute for alertness.
- Hike with a large group and stay together.
- Don't hike alone in bear country.
- Stay on the trail.
- Hike in the middle of the day.
- Make lots of noise while hiking.
- Never approach a bear.
- Female bears with cubs are very dangerous.
- Stay away from carcasses.
- Defensive hiking works. Try it.

be knowledgeable and then decide how far you want to go. Everybody has to make their own personal choice.

Here's another conflict: If you do everything listed here, you most likely will not see any bears—or any deer or moose or eagles or any other wildlife. Again, you make the choice. If you want to be as safe as possible, follow these rules religiously. If you want to see wildlife, including bears, do all of this in reverse, but then you are increasing your chance of an encounter instead of decreasing it.

Be Mountain Lion Aware, Too

The most important safety element for recreation in mountain lion country is simply recognizing their habitat. Mountain lions primarily feed on deer, so these common ungulates are a key element in cougar habitat. Fish and wildlife agencies usually have good information about deer distribution from population surveys and hunting results.

Basically, where you have a high deer population, you can expect to find mountain lions. If you are not familiar with identifying deer tracks, seek the advice of someone knowledgeable, or refer to a book on animal tracks such as the FalconGuide Scats and Tracks series.

To stay as safe as possible when hiking in mountain lion country, follow this advice.

- Travel with a friend or group. There's safety in numbers, so stay together.
- Don't let small children wander away by themselves.
- Don't let pets run unleashed.
- Avoid hiking at dawn and dusk—the times mountain lions are most active.

- Watch for warning signs of mountain lion activity such as cougar tracks or high deer numbers.
- Know how to behave if you encounter a mountain lion.

What to Do If You Encounter a Mountain Lion

In the vast majority of mountain lion encounters, the animals exhibit avoidance, indifference, or curiosity that does not result in human injury. But it is natural to be alarmed if you have an encounter of any kind. Try to keep your cool and consider the following:

Recognize threatening mountain lion behavior: There are a few cues that may help you gauge the risk of attack. If a mountain lion is more than 50 yards away, and it directs its attention to you, it may be only curious. This situation represents only a slight risk for adults, but a more serious risk to unaccompanied children. At this point, you should move away, while keeping the animal in your peripheral vision. Also, look for rocks, sticks, or something else to use as a weapon, just in case. If you have pepper spray, get it ready to discharge. If a mountain lion is crouched and staring intensely at you less than 50 yards away, it may be assessing the chances of a successful attack. If this behavior continues, the risk of attack may be high.

Do not approach a mountain lion: Instead, give the animal the opportunity to move on. Slowly back away, but maintain eye contact if close. Mountain lions are not known to attack humans to defend young or a kill, but they have been reported to "charge" in rare instances and may want to stay in the area. It's best to choose another route or time to hike through the area.

Do not run from a mountain lion: Running may stimulate a predatory response, and you won't be able to outrun them anyway.

Make noise: If you encounter a mountain lion, be vocal and talk or yell loudly and regularly. Try not to panic. Shout to make others in the area aware of the situation.

Maintain eye contact: Eye contact presents a challenge to the mountain lion, showing you are aware of its presence. Eye contact also helps you know where it is. However, if the behavior of the mountain lion is not threatening (if it is, for example, grooming or periodically looking away), maintain visual contact through your peripheral vision and move away.

Appear larger than you are: Raise your arms above your head and make steady waving motions. Raise your jacket or another object above your head. Do not bend over, as this will make you appear smaller and more "prey-like."

Grab the kids: If you are with small children, pick them up. First, bring children close to you, maintain eye contact with the mountain lion, and pull the children up without bending over. If you are with older children or adults, band together.

Defend yourself: If attacked, fight back. Try to remain standing. Do not feign death. Pick up a branch or rock; pull out a knife, pepper spray, or other deterrent device. Remember that everything is a potential weapon, and individuals have fended off mountain lions with blows from rocks, tree limbs, and even cameras.

Defend others: Also defend your hiking partners, but don't defend your pet. In past attacks on children, adults have successfully stopped attacks. However, such cases are very dangerous and risky, and physically defending a pet is not recommended.

Respect any warning signs posted by agencies.

Spread the word: Before leaving on your hike, discuss lions and teach others in your group how to behave in case of a mountain lion encounter. For example, anyone who starts running could bring on an attack.

Report encounters: If you have an encounter with a mountain lion, record your location and the details of the encounter, and notify the nearest landowner or land-management agency. The agency (federal, state, or county) may want to visit the site and, if appropriate, post education/ warning signs. Fish and wildlife agencies should also be notified because they record and track such encounters. If physical injury occurs, it is important to leave the area and not disturb the site of attack. Mountain lions that have attacked people must be killed, and an undisturbed site is critical for effectively locating the dangerous mountain lion.

How to Get Really Aware

Most of the information in this book comes from *Bear Aware* and *Lion Sense*, handy, inexpensive FalconGuides. These small, "packable" books contain the essential tips you need to reduce the risk of being injured by a bear or mountain lion to the slimmest possible margin, and they are written for both beginner and expert.

In addition to covering the all-important subject of how to prevent an encounter, these books include advice on what to do if you are involved in an encounter. Find copies at booksellers specializing in outdoor recreation and at national park visitor centers. You can order online at www.falcon.com.

The Beartooth Fishery

By Richard K. Stiff
Former High Mountain Lakes Survey Coordinator
Montana Department of Fish, Wildlife and Parks

The Absaroka-Beartooth Wilderness contains about 944 lakes, and of these, 328 support fisheries and 616 are barren. Only a few lakes in the entire wilderness (within the Slough Creek drainage) are thought to contain native fish, with surviving original Yellowstone cutthroat stock. All other fisheries within the wilderness were created when fish were introduced to lakes or streams. In some cases, introduced fish migrated and established populations in new locations. Lakes are currently managed by drainage due to the nature of the drainages and fish migration within each drainage, although this has not always been the case.

More than 60 percent of the lakes within the wilderness are barren of fish, their natural condition. These provide an opportunity for backcountry travelers to get away from anglers and find more solitude. While most anglers would probably enjoy seeing fish in many of these lakes, leaving them in their natural state is a tribute to the Absaroka-Beartooth as a true "wilderness." Without an environmental review, current laws prohibit the stocking of fish in lakes that have no history of a fishery.

The distribution of lakes (with and without fish) by drainage is:

Boulder River	103
Clarks Fork	426

East Rosebud	76
Rock Creek	91
Slough Creek	10
Stillwater River	154
West Rosebud	84
Total	**944**

The majority of the lakes are above 8,500 feet, with a number of these above 10,000 feet. Because of the high elevation, lakes often remain ice-covered until late June and have surface temperatures that seldom reach 60°F. The size of the fish in a lake is generally related to the size of the population. There are usually a few large fish, many medium-sized fish, or lots of smaller fish.

Lakes that harbor self-sustaining populations of fish often tend to become overpopulated, resulting in slower growth rates. Since brook trout have the least restrictive spawning requirements, they are most often the victims of poor growth rates. Lakes with brook trout tend to have stunted populations, although there are exceptions such as Cairn and Lower Aero Lakes.

Many of the lakes managed within the wilderness do not have a suitable place for trout to spawn and must be stocked to maintain a fishery. Most stocked lakes are planted with fish on a rotating cycle of three, four, six, and eight years, depending on use and management goals. Knowing the year these lakes are stocked can increase an angler's chance of catching good fish. Three- to four-year-old fish provide the best fishing for nice-sized trout.

Three- and four-year stocking cycles are generally used on lakes that receive significant fishing pressure and where a persistent good catch is desired. A six-year cycle allows at least some of the fish to grow larger, while still maintaining a constant fishery. Stocking at eight-year intervals is based on the premise that fish will live for seven years, and there will be a fallow year to allow the food population to recover. The eight-year cycle is used in lakes where a trophy-type fishery is desired, as well as in remote, relatively unproductive lakes. More lakes are being considered for the eight-year cycle.

There are many different species of fish in the Beartooths, although the majority of the lakes support only one species of fish. Cutthroat trout are the principal fish stocked because the area is in their original geographic range, and the hatchery in Big Timber provides an economical source of cutthroat trout. But many lakes were planted with brook trout in the first half of this century, and these have established populations.

Analysis of the fisheries reveals the following distribution of fish species:

Arctic grayling	11 lakes
Cutthroat trout	117 lakes
Eastern brook trout	85 lakes
Golden trout	25 lakes
Rainbow trout	22 lakes
Mixed fishery	56 lakes
Undecided	12 lakes
Total	**328 lakes**

Lake trout and brown trout are found in several mixed fisheries, mostly outside the wilderness boundaries.

Stream fisheries are different than lake fisheries. Since the Montana Department of Fish, Wildlife and Parks no longer plants fish in streams, the fish found there are self-supporting populations. Alpine streams, like alpine lakes, have a limited food supply. But in a stream the trout not only have to find food, they must also fight the current of the stream.

Trout rely on the current of the stream to bring food to them, while hiding from the current themselves. Places that do both of these things are at a premium, and the largest fish get the best spots. The number of good feeding spots and the amount of food available limit the number of fish that can be present in a given reach of stream. Streams tend to support fewer fish than lakes, but fish in streams are easier to locate. Anglers should note that stream and lake fishing regulations differ.

Trout can usually find suitable places to spawn in a stream, so reproduction is not a problem. The type of fish present usually reflects a combination of what was originally found in the stream, the fish that were planted, and the fish that have migrated down from lakes above.

One final note: The southeastern arm of the Beartooths straddles the border between Montana and Wyoming. Anglers in this area must be careful to fish only in the state for which they hold a valid fishing license. In some places, particularly where lakes actually straddle the border (as does Granite Lake, for example), it might be wise to carry licenses for both states. Also know and heed the appropriate regulations.

(For more information on the Absaroka-Beartooth fishery, get a copy of *Fishing the Beartooths* by Pat Marcuson. Also, check out an excellent website created by the Billings office of the Montana Department of Fish, Wildlife and Parks. Go to fwp.mt.gov and click on Mountain Lakes.)

Ranking the Hikes

The following list ranks the hikes in this book from easiest to hardest. No. 1 is the easiest, and No. 29 is the hardest. (Hike number follows in parentheses.)

1. Wild Bill Lake (9)
2. Crazy Creek Falls (23)
3. Night Lake (18)
4. Broadwater Lake (13)
5. Kersey Lake (24)
6. Pine Creek Falls (29)
7. Hauser Lake (17)
8. Passage Falls (28)
9. Woodbine Falls (4)
10. East Fork Boulder River (1)
11. Becker Lake (20)
12. Beauty Lake (21)
13. Gardner Lake (16)
14. Elk Lake (8)
15. Sioux Charley Lake (5)
16. Rock Island Lake (26)
17. West Stillwater (3)
18. Lake Vernon (25)
19. Slough Lake (7)
20. Lady of the Lake (27)
21. West Boulder Meadows (2)
22. Native Lake (22)
23. Basin Creek Lakes (10)
24. Glacier Lake (15)
25. Mystic Lake (6)
26. Timberline Lake (11)
27. West Fork of Rock Creek (12)
28. Beartooth High Lakes (19)
29. Hellroaring Plateau (14)

Map Legend

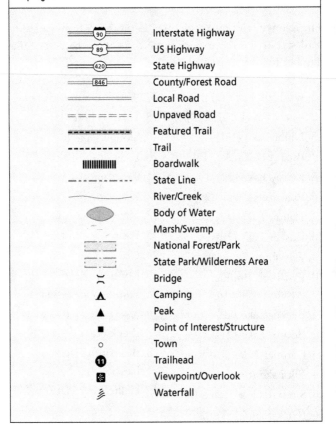

══🛡90══	Interstate Highway
══🛡89══	US Highway
══⬭420══	State Highway
══⬜846══	County/Forest Road
───────	Local Road
─ ─ ─ ─ ─	Unpaved Road
▪▪▪▪▪▪▪▪	Featured Trail
- - - - - -	Trail
▥▥▥▥▥▥	Boardwalk
— · · — · · —	State Line
⌇	River/Creek
⬭	Body of Water
	Marsh/Swamp
▢▢▢	National Forest/Park
▢▢▢	State Park/Wilderness Area
⌣⌒	Bridge
▲	Camping
▲	Peak
■	Point of Interest/Structure
○	Town
⓫	Trailhead
◈	Viewpoint/Overlook
⋙	Waterfall

1 East Fork Boulder River

An easy day hike along a beautiful stream with good fishing.

Start: Box Canyon Trailhead
Distance: 7.0 miles
out-and-back
Maps: USGS Mount Douglas
and Haystack Peak; RMS Mount

Douglas–Mount Wood and Cooke
City–Cutoff Mountain; and at
least one wilderness-wide map

Finding the trailhead: Drive 48 miles south from Big Timber on
Boulder River Road to the Box Canyon Trailhead, which is at the end
of the improved road. Large trailhead with toilets and plenty of parking most of the year, but can be crowded with horse trailers in September and October. GPS: 45.27344N / 110.25000W

The Hike

This trail is actually the "approach" to the popular routes into
Lake Plateau and Slough Creek. Consequently, even though
many people use this area, most hurry right through the East
Fork Boulder River on their way to somewhere else. This
makes it a pleasant day hike.

From the Box Canyon Trailhead, Trail 27 climbs gradually
along the East Fork. The trail stays a fair distance from the
river for about 3 miles. The first part of this trail was once a
wagon road, and it still looks like one. Fortunately, this isn't
because of heavy traffic, although the area receives moderate
use during July and August and heavy use from stock parties
in September during the early hunting season.

The trail leads to a great camping area about 3.5 miles
from the trailhead and then crosses the East Fork on a big

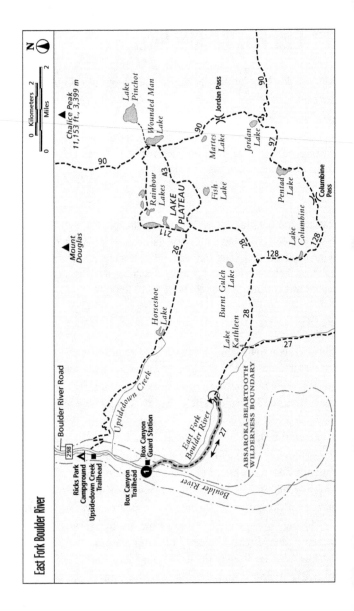

East Fork Boulder River

bridge. The large camping area just before the bridge can handle a large party or several parties. However, stock users should check the Forest Service regulations for the area (including group size limits) when planning to stay here.

Day hikers can easily spend a few hours fishing or lounging around this area, and even those bound for higher regions might want to linger. The stream is as charming as they get, and the fishing is great. The bridge marks a good turnaround point for day hikers.

Fishing

Above Box Canyon the East Fork Boulder River contains mostly cutthroat trout, although rainbows dominate the fishery below. Some of these cutthroats may be descendants of native stocks. A smattering of rainbows (immigrants from Rainbow Lakes above) can be found near where Rainbow Creek enters the East Fork Boulder River.

Cutthroat trout are aggressive and often easy to catch. As a result, where cutthroats dominate the fishery, fishing tends to be great. While this has been the fish's downfall in lower streams, most anglers in the Beartooths only keep enough for dinner, and populations seem stable.

None of the lakes near this route support a fishery, but Lake Kathleen provides an opportunity to observe a lake in its natural, untarnished state.

Miles and Directions

0.0 Start at Box Canyon Trailhead.

3.5 Bridge over East Fork Boulder River.

7.0 Arrive back at Box Canyon Trailhead.

2 West Boulder Meadows

An easy route along a scenic, fish-filled river.

Start: West Boulder Trailhead
Distance: 6.0 miles
out-and-back

Maps: USGS Mount Rae and Mt. Cowen; RMS Mount Cowen Area; and at least one wilderness-wide map

Finding the trailhead: Drive 18 miles south from Big Timber on Boulder River Road to about a half mile past McLeod, and cross the West Boulder River. About a half mile later, turn right (west) onto West Boulder Road, which starts as pavement but quickly turns to gravel. After 7.4 miles turn left (west) at a wellsigned junction, continuing on West Boulder Road. (Don't go straight here—it's private land. West Boulder Road also crosses private land, but it's a public road.) Drive 6.2 more miles until you see West Boulder Campground on your right. Park at the trailhead just past the campground entrance. Toilet in campground, but not at trailhead. The road continues on past the trailhead, but it's a private road, so don't drive on it. GPS: 45.54698N / 110.30740W

The Hike

One of the highlights of this hike is the drive to the trailhead. West Boulder Road winds through a scenic slice of the "real Montana"—wide-open spaces, snowcapped mountains, big valleys with rustic cattle ranches, aspens coloring the transitions between grassland and forest, and, of course, a beautiful stream all the way. If you drive to the trailhead near dawn or dusk, it resembles a video game trying to dodge all the deer on the road.

You can make this trip any length that suits you. It's 8 miles to the junction with the Falls Creek Trail, but there is no need to hike that far.

From the campground, hike up a dirt road, through an open gate, for about 100 yards. Then, watch for a sign on the left and a trail heading left to the sign. Turn left here. Don't continue on the road, which goes to a private residence. This is all private land, but the landowner has been cooperative in allowing public access. Please show your appreciation by respecting the landowner's private property rights.

The first part of the trail is very well constructed—raised, drained, graveled, lined with logs, a regular hiker's highway. About a half mile up the trail, you go through a gate. Be sure to lock it behind you. Just before the bridge over the West Boulder River (and another gate) about a mile down the trail, you enter the Absaroka-Beartooth Wilderness, where it becomes a normal trail.

The first mile is flat, but then you climb two switchbacks and get a good view of the river. From here the trail goes through a partially burned forest interspersed with gorgeous mountain meadows—and they're large, too, especially West Boulder Meadows. Several of the meadows have excellent campsites, and the river offers good fishing all the way. After West Boulder Meadows, you can see a beautiful waterfall.

This hike provides a reminder that wilderness is a multiple-use land designation with livestock grazing allowed. A local rancher holds a grazing allotment in West Boulder Meadows. You'll see an unsightly steel-post fence at the west end of the meadows, very out of character for the surroundings. And, of course, expect to see a few cows and cow pies.

The entire trail is in great shape, with a gradual stream-grade incline all the way. Unlike many trails, this one stays by

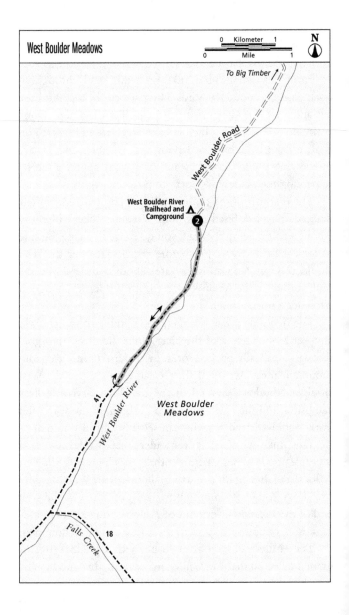

West Boulder Meadows

0 Kilometer 1

0 Mile 1

N

To Big Timber

West Boulder Road

West Boulder River
Trailhead and
Campground

2

41

West Boulder River

West Boulder
Meadows

Falls Creek

18

the stream most of the way. Recent forest fires, however, have burned large sections of the valley.

Fishing

In the lower stretches of the river, you can catch cutthroats, rainbows, or browns, but as you proceed upstream and get close to the Falls Creek junction, it's mostly cutts.

Miles and Directions

0.0 Start at West Boulder Trailhead.

0.25 Trail turns off private road; turn left.

1.0 Bridge over West Boulder River and wilderness boundary.

3.0 West Boulder Meadows.

6.0 Arrive back at West Boulder Trailhead.

3 West Stillwater

A great hike for hikers wanting to experience a remote uncrowded wilderness river valley.

Start: West Stillwater Trailhead
Distance: Varies; up to 16 miles out-and-back

Maps: USGS Picket Pin Mountain and Tumble Mountain; RMS Mount Douglas–Mount Wood; and at least one wilderness-wide map

---

Finding the trailhead: From I-90 at Columbus, Montana, drive 15 miles south on MT 78 to Absarokee. Continue south from town about 2 miles and turn right on the Nye Road (County Road 419). Drive about 25 miles southwest, through Nye, to the Stillwater Mine (which is about 2 miles before the Stillwater River Trailhead and Woodbine Campground at road's end). Immediately after the mine, turn right (west) on Forest Road 846 (on the map) or 2846 (on the sign) at a well-marked intersection. From here, it's a long, bumpy 8.6 miles to the trailhead. Initial Creek Campground is about a mile before the end of the road. Drive past the campground to the very end of the road. Ample parking for hikers (stock users have a separate trailhead about a half mile before the hiker's trailhead), toilet. GPS: 45.39710N / 109.96892W

The Hike

Unlike the Stillwater River Trailhead, one of the most accessible and heavily used access points to the Beartooths, the West Stillwater receives very little use. You can start this hike at the trailhead, of course, but if you're camped at the Initial Creek Campground, you can also take a scenic trail directly from the campground for about a mile along the river to the official trailhead.

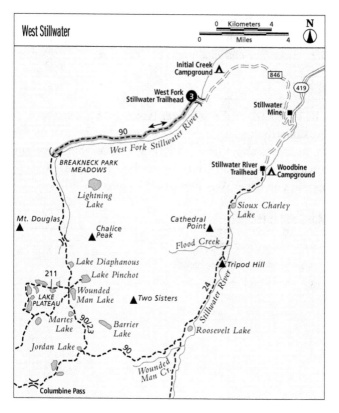

The trail eventually goes all the way to the Lake Plateau, passing by Breakneck Park Meadows at the 8-mile mark, but you don't have to go nearly that far. You can hike a mile or two or more, as far as you want, up the gradual grade along the West Fork Stillwater River and then return to the trailhead. You can expect excellent trail conditions all the way.

The well-maintained trail closely follows the West Fork Stillwater River, hugging the north and west bank. As you proceed up the trail, you go through several small meadows.

After going as far as you like, relax for a while, and then enjoy the gradual downhill hike back to the trailhead. Watch for deer, moose, or elk, all abundant in the area.

Fishing

The West Fork of the Stillwater River harbors a mixed fishing opportunity. The lower reaches have brown trout, brook trout, and rainbow trout. The browns phase out upstream, leaving rainbows and brookies, while cutthroats start to appear. The upper West Fork contains mostly cutthroats.

Miles and Directions

- **0.0** Start at West Stillwater Trailhead.
- **8.0** Breakneck Park Meadows.
- **16.0** Arrive back at West Stillwater Trailhead.

4 Woodbine Falls

A short day hike to an amazing waterfall.

Start: Woodbine Falls Trailhead in Woodbine Campground
Distance: 3.0 miles out-and-back

Maps: USGS Cathedral Point; RMS Mount Douglas–Mount Wood; and at least 1 wilderness-wide map

Finding the trailhead: From I-90 at Columbus, drive 15 miles south on MT 78 to Absarokee. Continue south 2 miles, turn west onto the paved Nye Road (CR 419), and go through Fishtail and Nye. Stay on this road, which eventually ends at the trailhead, about 2 miles past the Stillwater Mine to Woodbine Campground. It's about 42 miles southwest of Columbus. Plenty of parking and a toilet. GPS: 45.35082N / 109.90331W

Author's note: The 2022 flood washed out the bridge over Woodbine Creek, and it might be several years before it is replaced. Hikers can still reach Woodbine Falls by carefully fording the creek just downstream from the trail or, also carefully, crossing on a downed tree just upstream from the trail. Check with the Forest Service or the camp host at Woodbine Campground for the status of the bridge replacement.

The Hike

Woodbine Falls is one of the most heavily traveled trails in the Beartooths. The majority of people staying at Woodbine Campground probably take this hike since they can walk to the trailhead from their campsite.

From the trailhead, hike about a quarter mile to Wood-bine Creek and cross the bridge. From here you hike up five

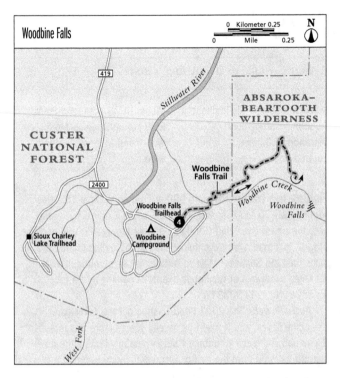

or six nicely engineered switchbacks to an overlook where you can take in the majestic of Woodbine Falls. The trail is in great shape the entire way, with the added touch of masonry on some switchbacks and at the overlook.

The earlier in the season you can take this hike, the more majestic the falls. Snow usually departs this area earlier than in the high country, so you probably can do this hike in June during the spring runoff.

Getting a good photo of the falls is difficult because of trees blocking part of the view, but it's still a very impressive view.

No camping is allowed on this route except in Woodbine Campground.

Miles and Directions

0.0 Start at Woodbine Falls Trailhead.

0.3 Woodbine Creek.

1.5 Woodbine Falls.

3.0 Arrive back at Woodbine Falls Trailhead.

5 Sioux Charley Lake

A short hike along a wilderness river to a fish–filled lake.

Start: Stillwater/Sioux Charley Trailhead

Distance: 8.0 miles out-and-back

Maps: USGS Cathedral Point; RMS Mount Douglas–Mount Wood; and at least 1 wilderness-wide map

Finding the trailhead: From I-90 at Columbus, drive 15 miles south on MT 78 to Absarokee. Continue south 2 miles, turn west onto the paved Nye Road (CR 419), and go through Fishtail and Nye. Stay on this road, which eventually ends at the trailhead, about 2 miles past the Stillwater Mine. It's about 42 miles southwest of Columbus. Plenty of parking and toilet; Woodbine Campground is near the trailhead. GPS: 45.35082N / 109.90331W

Author's note: This area was severely impacted by the 2022 flooding, but the Stillwater/Sioux Charley Trailhead reopened for the summer of 2023. However, the trailhead parking lot was destroyed, so hikers might need to park along the road near the trailhead. The flood washed out the first part of the trail through a rocky gorge, but hikers can take the stock bypass trail from the trailhead, which connects to the main trail just beyond the gorge. The distance is about the same, but hikers have to climb a steep hill on the bypass trail instead of enjoying the fairly flat section of trail through the gorge. The trail up this hill was made for horses, not hikers, so it's steeper than normal. It might be several years before the gorge section is replaced.

The Hike

This easy day trip into Sioux Charley Lake is one of the most popular day hikes in the Beartooths, so don't be surprised to see lots of people on the trail. From the trailhead it's 3 miles to the lake, all on an easy and gradual river grade.

Soon after leaving the trailhead, the trail enters a narrow canyon where, right next to the trail, the Stillwater River tumbles over a series of cascades and rapids. Many a hiker has paused here to wonder why this stream was ever named the "still water."

After passing through the canyon, the trail winds through a heavy forest all the way to Sioux Charley Lake. Now the reason behind the river's name becomes clear. The lake is really just a large, slowmoving, or "still," section of the river. Farther upstream, the river slows into several similar still-water stretches.

Look across the lake to the east to see the northernmost reaches of the dramatic forest fires of 1988. The massive Storm Creek Fire burned all the way down the Stillwater River drainage to Sioux Charley Lake, almost completely through the Beartooths.

Fishing

The Stillwater River can yield a lot of pan-size trout, a mix of rainbows and brookies, plus an occasional cutthroat. Brookies dominate the slower water, with rainbows and cutts liking the faster water. Since brook trout tend to overpopulate (to the detriment of other species), please eat them to help out the cutts and rainbows. Catch-and-release doesn't improve the brookies' size; it only limits the amount of food available per fish. Besides, they taste great! Sioux Charley Lake is one of the best places to catch these tasty morsels, and they can provide dinner for many large parties with no impact on the health of the population.

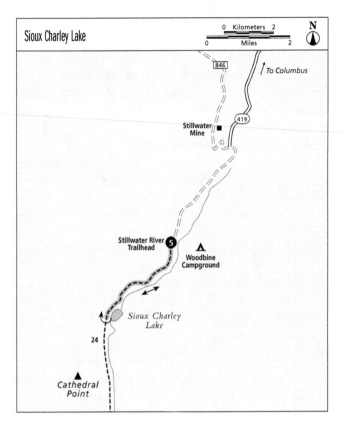

Miles and Directions

0.0 Start at Stillwater/Sioux Charley Trailhead.

4.0 Sioux Charley Lake.

8.0 Arrive back at Stillwater/Sioux Charley Trailhead.

6 Mystic Lake

A day trip to the deepest lake in the Beartooths.

Start: West Rosebud Trailhead
Distance: 7.0 miles
out-and-back

Maps: USGS Granite Peak and
Alpine; RMS Cooke City-Cutoff
Mountain; and at least one
wilderness-wide map

Finding the trailhead: From 1-90 at Columbus, drive 15 miles
south on MT 78 through Absarokee. About 2 miles past Absarokee,
turn right (west) onto CR 419. Drive through Fishtail and continue
west and south about 1 mile, then turn left (south) along West Rosebud Road. About 6 miles later, take another left (southeast) at the
sign for West Rosebud Lake (pavement ends). From here it's another
14.4 miles of bumpy gravel road to the trailhead—a total of 26 miles
from Absarokee and 41 miles from Columbus. The road ends and
the trail starts at the Mystic Dam Power Station. Ample parking (but
sometimes packed) and toilet; two developed campgrounds on the
way to the trailhead. GPS: 45.22782N / 109.76183W

The Hike

For those who aren't interested in strenuous mountain
climbing or long arduous adventures, the Mystic Lake trail
offers an excellent choice for an unhurried day into the
wilderness. It also offers some spectacular scenery with the
unusual twist of being able to observe the Mystic Lake Power
Station. Besides being a popular day trip, the trail to Mystic
Lake is also the first leg for the legions heading up to attempt
an ascent of Granite Peak, Montana's highest, so don't expect
to have the trail to yourself. As a small added bonus, you

won't have to step over any horse apples on this trail. Horse use is prohibited on the section of trail between the power station and Mystic Lake during the hiking season but allowed during the fall hunting season.

A short way up the trail, look for a plaque placed in a stone in memory of Mark E. Von Seggern, a Boy Scout from Columbus who died in 1979 after a tragic slide down a snowbank near Mystic Lake.

From the trailhead, follow West Rosebud Creek. After crossing a bridge over the creek, the trail follows a power line for a short way. After leaving behind these "signs of civilization," you switchback through open rock fields that offer a great view of the West Rosebud valley, including West Rosebud and Emerald Lakes.

The climb doesn't seem that steep, but by the time the trail reaches the dam at the eastern end of Mystic Lake, it has ascended 1,200 feet in 3 miles. Normally that would be considered a big climb, but for hikers who aren't in a hurry, it really doesn't seem like it.

When you finally break out over the ridge, you're treated to a sweeping view of Mystic Lake and Mystic Dam. Mystic Lake is a natural lake, but the dam increased its size and depth—now at more than 200 feet deep, the deepest lake in the Beartooths.

The sandy beach along the east shore of the lake below is perhaps the largest in the Beartooths. This makes a good lunch spot for those who plan to turn back for the trailhead. But it's far better to set aside enough time to walk along the lake for a while. The trail is very scenic, flat, and well maintained. Plus, it's difficult to realize the full scope of Mystic Lake from the first overlook. This is a huge lake, and a walk along its shore is the best way to appreciate it.

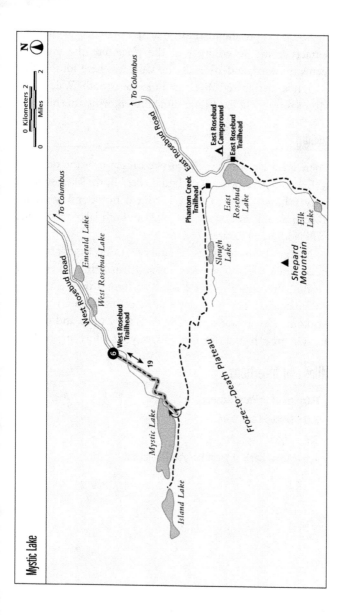

Mystic Lake

Some people might think that the presence of the dam detracts from the wildness of the place, but the intrusion seems minimal, and after all, the dam was here long before Congress designated the Absaroka-Beartooth Wilderness. Most visitors will have little difficulty enjoying this hike.

Fishing

There are a lot of fish willing to be caught near the trailhead at Emerald and West Rosebud Lakes. Both lakes support hefty fish, with brown trout, cutthroat trout, and whitefish all common. Rainbows are stocked in both lakes to provide some additional excitement.

Mystic Lake supports a rainbow trout fishery that is great when the fish are feeding and frustrating when they are not, although the fickle rainbows found there can usually be coaxed. The rainbows can be counted on for a good workout. The stream up to Mystic is very steep and doesn't provide great habitat for fish, so save your effort for the lake.

Miles and Directions

- **0.0** Start at West Rosebud Trailhead.
- **3.0** Mystic Lake Dam.
- **3.5** Mystic Lake.
- **7.0** Arrive back at West Rosebud Trailhead.

7 Slough Lake

A leisurely day trip with a terrific view of the upper Phantom Creek drainage and Froze-to-Death Plateau.

Start: Phantom Creek Trailhead
Distance: 4.0 miles
out-and-back

Maps: USGS Alpine; RMS Alpine-Mount Maurice; and at least one wilderness-wide map

---

Finding the Trailhead: To find the Phantom Creek Trailhead, from I-90 at Columbus, Montana, go south 29 miles on MT 78 to Roscoe. Drive through this small ranching community, being careful not to stop at the Grizzly Bar—until the return trip, of course, when you'll be really ready for the famous Grizzly Burger. At the north end of Roscoe, the road turns to gravel and goes about 14.5 miles to the East Rosebud Trailhead. About 7 miles from Roscoe, the road crosses East Rosebud Creek and forks. Take a sharp right and continue south along the creek. The road is mostly gravel, except for a 4-mile paved section near the end. Phantom Creek Trail 17 begins on the right (west) side of the road a quarter mile before East Rosebud Lake. Ample parking; toilet; and large vehicle campground nearby. GPS: 45.24574N / 109.72990W

The Hike

This trail is perfectly suited for a leisurely, quiet day in the wilderness amid some great scenery.

Trail 17 climbs, with gradual switchbacks, westerly along Armstrong Creek for about 2 miles to Slough Lake. This is a gorgeous, glacier-carved cirque, and Slough Lake sits in the midst of it like a little pearl. Actually, there are two small lakes.

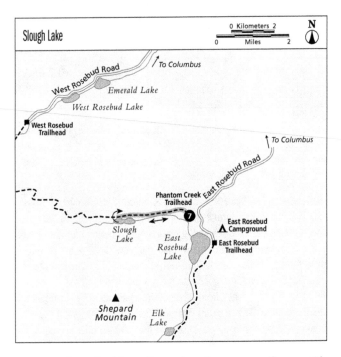

Even though this trail receives heavy use, few people take their time along here or even stop at Slough Lake. Most are rushing to the top of Froze-to-Death Plateau to climb Granite Peak. Lucky for the rest of us that they hurry by this pastoral pond, a perfect spot to sit on a sunny day savoring the spirit of the wilderness.

If you want a little more exercise, hike about another half mile until the trail breaks out of the forest. This gives you a truly spectacular vista highlighted by Hole-in-the-Wall Mountain to the left (south) and Froze-to-Death Plateau to the west.

Fishing

Slough Lake provides a good source of willing brookies for dinner.

Miles and Directions

0.0 Start at Phantom Creek Trailhead.

2.0 Slough Lake.

4.0 Arrive back at Phantom Creek Trailhead.

8 Elk Lake

A fairly easy day trip to a fish-filled mountain lake.

Start: East Rosebud Trailhead
Distance: 6.0 miles
out-and-back

Maps: USGS Alpine; RMS Alpine-
Mount Maurice; and at least one
wilderness-wide map

Finding the trailhead: From I-90 at Columbus, Montana, drive
south 29 miles on MT 78 to Roscoe. Drive through this small ranching community, being careful not to stop at the Grizzly Bar—until the
return trip, of course, when you'll be really ready for the famous Grizzly
Burger. At the north end of Roscoe, the road turns to gravel and goes
about 14 miles to the East Rosebud Trailhead, the first 2 miles paved.
About 3.5 miles from Roscoe, the road crosses East Rosebud Creek
and forks. Take a sharp right and continue south along the creek. The
road is mostly gravel with a 4-mile paved section. A huge parking lot
with toilet and room for large horse trailers; a large vehicle campground nearby. GPS: 45.19727N / 109.63520W

The Hike

This trail covers the first 3 miles of the popular trans-
Beartooth trail from East Rosebud to Clarks Fork, often
referred to as the Beaten Path. The trail is well maintained
and well traveled. Expect to see lots of people.

The trail starts at the huge East Rosebud Trailhead and
goes through a forested valley all the way to Elk Lake. In
1996 a forest fire burned through here, so expect to see the
aftermath of the fire.

Along the trail you can also get several great views of
10,979-foot Shepard Mountain to the west and of East

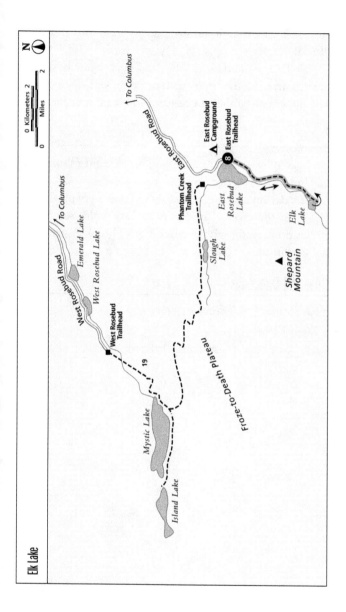

Elk Lake

N

0 Kilometers 2
0 Miles 2

To Columbus

East Rosebud Road

East Rosebud Campground

East Rosebud Trailhead

8

Phantom Creek Trailhead

East Rosebud Lake

Slough Lake

Elk Lake

Shepard Mountain

Froze-to-Death Plateau

To Columbus

West Rosebud Road

Emerald Lake

West Rosebud Lake

West Rosebud Trailhead

19

Mystic Lake

Island Lake

Rosebud Creek as it tumbles down from the Beartooth Plateau.

Elk Lake is nestled in a forested pocket just below the point where the trail starts to traverse rockier, open terrain. The upper end of the lake features a pleasant spot for lunch.

Fishing

Elk Lake offers both cutthroat and brook trout fishing, with the brook trout providing the best possibility for dinner. Anglers day hiking to Elk Lake should plan a couple of stops to fish in the creek. East Rosebud Lake holds some large brown trout, along with a mixed bag of brookies, rainbows, and cutthroats.

Miles and Directions

0.0 Start at East Rosebud Trailhead.

3.0 Elk Lake.

6.0 Arrive back at East Rosebud Trailhead.

9 Wild Bill Lake

A very easy day loop around a charming little lake.

Start: Wild Bill Lake Campground
Distance: 1.0-mile loop

Maps: USGS Alpine; RMS Alpine–
Mount Maurice; and at least one
wilderness-wide map

Finding the trailhead: From I-90 at Laurel, drive south on US 212
about 45 miles to the south side of Red Lodge. Turn west on the West
Fork of Rock Creek Road (Forest Road 71). After 2.7 miles, the road
bends left and heads up the West Fork. After driving another 3.3 miles
on the paved road, turn right (north) into the well-signed parking lot
for Wild Bill Lake. GPS: 45.15518N / 109.36742W

The Hike

Wild Bill Lake was built by "Wild Bill" Kurtzer with a hand-
built dam. He stocked fish in the small lake and rented fishing
boats to tourists. He built quite a commercial venture and
even had a heated swimming hole.

A delightful short trail follows the shoreline all around
Wild Bill Lake. Part of the trail is accessible to wheelchairs.
This is a terrific short hike for people with small children.

Fishing

Some fishing for stocked rainbows. It's a nice place to let the
kids give fishing a try.

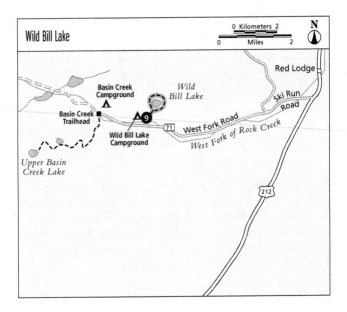

10 Basin Creek Lakes

An easy day hike well suited for families on a designated National Recreation Trail.

Start: Basin Creek Trailhead
Distance: 5.0 miles out-and-back to lower lake; 8.0 miles out-and-back to upper lake

Maps: USGS Bare Mountain; RMS Alpine–Mount Maurice; and at least one wilderness-wide map

Finding the trailhead: Once in Red Lodge, go to the north edge of town and watch for the big sign for the Red Lodge Mountain Ski Resort and take a right (west) onto the West Fork Road (also called Ski Run Road and Forest Road 71). When the road forks at 3 miles, take the left fork, staying on the paved West Fork Road and not the gravel road continuing on up to the ski resort. The road is paved until you reach the Basin Creek Campground, where it turns into a good gravel road. The trailhead is on your left just before the campground. Fairly large parking lot and a toilet. Vehicle camping at nearby Basin Creek and Cascade Campgrounds. GPS 45.15922N / 109.38926W

The Hike

The Forest Service has designated Basin Creek Lakes as a National Recreation Trail, so, not surprisingly, it's popular. It's so popular, in fact, that this is one of the few trails in the Beartooths restricted to hiking only—no horses are allowed until mid-September when the big-game hunting seasons get underway.

Technically, Trail 61 to Basin Creek Lakes doesn't pass through the Absaroka-Beartooth Wilderness, but it's a wilderness trip by all other definitions. The trail is well maintained, easy to follow, and ideal for family day trips for anyone who can handle a gradual but steady uphill gradient. The route crosses Basin Creek on a bridge.

About a half mile up the trail, listen for Basin Creek Falls tumbling down from above. Where the trail takes a sharp right, hikers can scramble up a short, undeveloped spur trail to get a closer look at the falls, which is well worth the short detour. The rest of the trail is hazard-free, but this short climb up to see the falls might be too hazardous for small children.

The trail passes through thick forest all the way to the lakes with the exception of a short burned section near the trailhead. With so much of the Beartooths burned by recent fires, this peaceful walk in the woods can be a real treat. You can still see the remains of logging activity from the early 1900s along the way—and how nature has mostly reclaimed the disturbed landscape.

Lower Basin Creek Lake is one of those forest-lined mountain ponds with darkish, warm water that tends to be half-covered with lily pads. Upper Basin Creek Lake is larger, deeper, and nestled in a picturesque mountain cirque.

Fishing

While both of these lakes once supported brook trout populations, the lower lake suffered a freeze-out a few years back and currently has no fish. Since the brook trout in the stream and lake above will eventually work their way back down to Lower Basin, there is no immediate need to restock. Fishing in Upper Basin Lake is excellent for brook trout, and there has been some talk of introducing grayling.

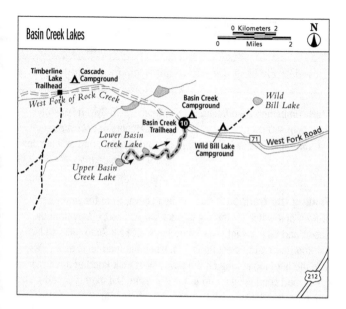

Basin Creek Lakes

Miles and Directions

0.0   Start at Basin Creek Trailhead.

0.5   Basin Creek Falls.

2.5   Lower Basin Creek Lake.

4.0   Upper Basin Creek Lake.

8.0   Arrive back at Basin Creek Trailhead.

11 Timberline Lake

A moderately long day trip to an idyllic mountain lake.

Start: Timberline Lake Trailhead
Distance: 9.0 miles
out-and-back

Maps: USGS Sylvan Peak and
Bare Mountain; RMS Alpine–
Mount Maurice; and at least one
wilderness-wide map

Finding the trailhead: Once in Red Lodge, go to the north edge
of town and watch for the big sign for the Red Lodge Mountain Ski
Resort and take a right (west) onto the West Fork Road (also called
Ski Run Road and Forest Road 71). When the road forks at 3 miles,
take the left fork, staying on the paved West Fork Road and not the
gravel road continuing on up to the ski resort. The road is paved until
you reach the Basin Creek Campground, where it turns into a good
gravel road. Go 4 more miles and turn left (south) into the Timberline
Lake Trailhead (11 miles total from Red Lodge), which has a fairly
large parking lot (but too small for horse trailers) and a toilet. GPS:
45.17180N / 109.46017W

The Hike

Similar to the nearby trail up Basin Creek, the trail to Timberline Lake passes through a forested environment. Unlike
Basin Creek, much of this route burned when the 2008 Cascade Fire swept through the upper West Fork Valley. As with
almost all trails in this section of the Absaroka-Beartooth
Wilderness, this one is well maintained and marked.

The corridor to Timberline Lake was excluded from the
Absaroka-Beartooth Wilderness. However, Lake Gertrude
and Timberline Lake lie within the wilderness boundary.

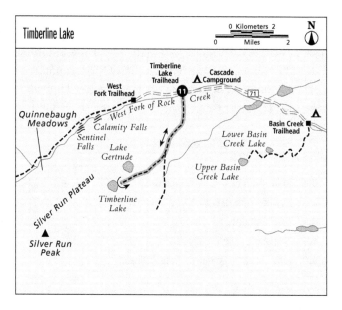

It's a short 3 miles to the junction with Silver Run Lakes Trail 18, which veers off to the left and heads up to Silver Run Plateau. Turn right and continue along Timberline Creek. If you cross the stream here, you took a wrong turn.

After another mile or so, look for Lake Gertrude off to the right. This is a good spot to pause for a rest while enjoying the lake, which also marks the boundary of the Absaroka-Beartooth Wilderness. Don't burn too much daylight here, however. Timberline Lake is only 0.5 mile farther, and you'll want to leave time to explore this high-altitude basin.

The view from Timberline Lake is fantastic, especially to the south toward Timberline Glacier and 12,500-foot Silver Run Peak.

Fishing

Both lakes along this trail have healthy populations of brook trout. The fish aren't large but can probably be counted on to provide dinner. The small outlet ponds below Timberline Lake may prove an easier place to catch fish than the lake itself.

Miles and Directions

0.0 Start at Timberline Lake Trailhead.

3.0 Junction with Beartrack Trail 8; turn right.

4.0 Lake Gertrude.

4.5 Timberline Lake.

9.0 Arrive back at Timberline Lake Trailhead.

12 West Fork of Rock Creek

A fairly flat route to expansive meadows, passing by two waterfalls on the way.

Start: West Fork Trailhead
Distance: Varies; up to 10 miles out-and-back

Maps: USGS Sylvan Peak and Bare Mountain; RMS Alpine– Mount Maurice; and at least one wilderness-wide map

Finding the trailhead: Once in Red Lodge, go to the north edge of town and watch for the big sign for the Red Lodge Mountain Ski Resort and take a right (west) onto the West Fork Road (also called Ski Run Road and Forest Road 71). When the road forks at 3 miles, take the left fork, staying on the paved West Fork Road and not the gravel road continuing on up to the ski resort. The road is paved until you reach the Basin Creek Campground, where it turns into a good gravel road. From here, you have about 6 more miles of gravel to the end of the road and the West Fork Trailhead, which has a fairly large parking lot and a toilet. GPS: 45.16835N / 109.59605W

The Hike

You can make this hike as long or as short as you want. You can keep it to about 4 miles by seeing the two waterfalls and then call it a day, or you can go all the way to Quinnebaugh Meadows.

The trail, like others in this region, is well maintained and marked. It closely follows the West Fork of Rock Creek, a gradual stream grade all the way to Quinnebaugh Meadows. Most of the trail passes through a rich forest that gradually thins out as you progress up the drainage, parts of it burned

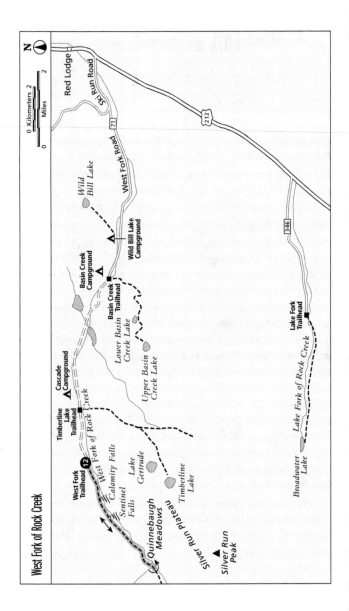

West Fork of Rock Creek

by the 2008 Cascade Fire. In a few places the forest opens up into small meadows with rewarding vistas of Elk Mountain and Bowback Mountain on the southern horizon near the terminus of the West Fork valley.

The trail passes close by Calamity Falls and Sentinel Falls. These cascades are reminders that the West Fork is not only a peaceful stream meandering out of the wilderness, but that it can be a powerful force as well. Short spur trails lead to both falls for better views.

The West Fork broadens out and slows down just as the trail nears Quinnebaugh Meadows. Look for the sign for Lake Mary just after breaking out into the enormous mountain meadow. This is a popular place, so expect company.

Fishing

Although the West Fork of Rock Creek is not highly productive, anglers can find a few trout in many stretches of this stream. The stream near Quinnebaugh Meadows is no exception. The best fishing, however, is found in various basin lakes 1,000 feet higher in elevation.

Miles and Directions

- **0.0** Start at West Fork Trailhead.
- **1.3** Calamity Falls.
- **1.8** Sentinel Falls.
- **5.0** Quinnebaugh Meadows and junction with Lake Mary Trail.
- **10.0** Arrive back at West Fork Trailhead.

13 Broadwater Lake

An easy day trip to a small in-stream lake.

Start: Lake Fork Trailhead
Distance: Up to 7.0 miles
out-and-back

Maps: USGS Black Pyramid
Mountain; RMS Alpine–Mount
Maurice; and at least one
wilderness-wide map

Finding the trailhead: From Red Lodge, drive southwest for 9
miles on US 212. Turn west at the well-marked road up the Lake Fork
of Rock Creek. A 2-mile paved road leads to a turnaround and the
trailhead. A huge trailhead area with plenty of parking and room for
horse trailers, but even this large lot gets full on busy weekends; toilet.
GPS: 45.07915N / 109.41104W

The Hike

From the trailhead, immediately cross a bridge over the Lake
Fork of Rock Creek, turn right (west), and head upstream
along the Lake Fork. The trail stays close to the stream all the
way and is easy to follow, well maintained, hazard-free, and
usually dry. Plus, there are no steep hills, and the trail stays
on the south side of the stream the entire way to Broadwater
Lake with one easy stream crossing.

All of these advantages make this trip near-perfect for an
easy day hike with children. Perhaps the best part of the trip
to Broadwater Lake is constantly being near a clean, natural
mountain stream. Hikers can stop at dozens of places and
just sit back against a tree, relax, and soak in the sound of the
rushing water. Along the way watch for water ouzels playing

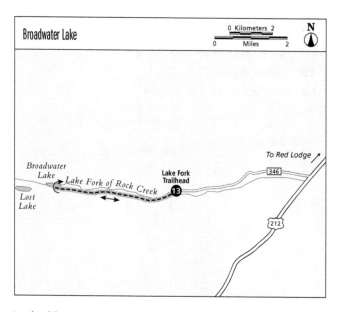

Broadwater Lake

0 Kilometers 2

0 Miles 2

N

To Red Lodge

346

Broadwater Lake

Lake Fork of Rock Creek

Lost Lake

Lake Fork Trailhead

13

212

in the bluegreen waters of the Lake Fork and expect to see lots of wildflowers along the stream.

Broadwater Lake is beautiful, but it's not well named. It's not really a lake at all but a long "glide" where the stream widens and slows for a few moments before continuing to hurry out of the mountains.

Fishing

Like the West Fork, the Lake Fork of Rock Creek is exceptionally photogenic, but it supports fewer fish than might be expected. The cold water, restricted sunlight, and fast current don't make life easy for fish. The Lake Fork supports both cutthroat and brook trout, but with some exceptions, the numbers are not high. Fish concentrate in the slower sections of the stream, and Broadwater Lake is one of these.

Miles and Directions

0.0   Start at Lake Fork Trailhead.

3.5   Broadwater Lake.

7.0   Arrive back at Lake Fork Trailhead.

14 Hellroaring Plateau

A short, mostly off-trail trip into a high-elevation basin filled with lakes.

Start: Hellroaring Plateau Trailhead

Distance: 4 to 8 miles, depending on how much exploring you do; out-and-back with loop option

Maps: USGS Black Pyramid Mountain, RMS Alpine–Mount Maurice; and at least one wilderness-wide map

Finding the trailhead: A big part of this hike is the adventure you'll have driving to the trailhead, a 2-hour drive each way. Drive south from Red Lodge on US 212 for 10.9 miles. Watch for a well-marked turnoff on the right (west) to three Forest Service campgrounds. Stay on this paved road for 0.9 mile until you cross a bridge near the entrance to Limberpine Campground. Immediately after the bridge, the pavement ends and you reach a fork in the road. For the Hellroaring Plateau, turn right (north, then sharply turn southwest). You definitely need a high-clearance four-wheel-drive vehicle or an ATV to get to this trailhead. Snow usually blocks this gravel road until at least early July. Once on the road to the Hellroaring Plateau Trailhead parking area, there's only one fork in the road, about a half mile before the trailhead where you go left. It's a rough 7 miles to the end of the road and the trailhead, which is on the edge of the Hellroaring Plateau. This road isn't for fainthearted drivers or horse trailers. Ample parking; no toilet. GPS: 45.03783N / 109.45190W

Author's note: The 2022 floods washed out a bridge on the Hellroaring Road, so the trailhead is not accessible with a motor vehicle. There is no timetable for replacing the bridge, so this road has become a hiking and biking trail, which is the only way to reach the Hellroaring Trailhead. ATVs can make it as far as where the bridge used to be, but there is very limited parking. Until the road becomes usable by high-clearance vehicles, this would not be considered a Best Easy Day Hike because hikers would have to add the road mileage to the hike route, making this a difficult trip. Check with the Forest Service for the current road status before trying this hike.

The Hike

The trails in this area are great for learning to explore the high country with a topographic map and compass or GPS unit, and they are especially well suited for hikers who aren't in top physical condition. Many lakes and other scenic areas can be reached within a few miles of the trailhead. The climbs can be steep but not extended.

From the trailhead, follow an old, closed-off jeep road about 1 mile along the Hellroaring Plateau. Lower Hellroaring Lakes are soon visible in the valley off to the right (north). You are better off continuing along the plateau instead of going down to the lakes from this point. If you drop off too early, the terrain gets very steep, and it's a fight through a maze of alpine willows and small streams.

Instead, continue along the plateau for another half mile or so. The scenery is worth it. Wander over to the south edge of the plateau on the left to see the main fork of Rock Creek.

At about the 1.5-mile mark and just before a huge snowbank on the right (northwest), head down to the lakes. Take a close look at the topo map before dropping off the plateau, and keep the map handy until you climb back out of the basin.

The climb down to the lakes is more gradual from this point. Watch for game trails on the way down, but be prepared for essentially off-trail hiking. Once at the lakes, the hiking is much easier. There are fairly well-defined anglers' trails between the lakes.

This is a heavenly basin filled with lakes, mostly above 10,000 feet. Hairpin Lake, for example, is definitely worth seeing. It has a series of beautiful bays, and a waterfall plunges into the lake from the northwest. There's plenty of grand places to explore, and all within a short distance.

After a few hours exploring the basin, climb back up to the plateau and hike back to your vehicle. To make a short loop out of the trip, hike down to the lower lakes and then up to the plateau. Bear in mind that the climb back to the plateau from the lower basin is tough. It's better to retrace your steps up the valley and then take the more gradual climb to the plateau just east of the large snowbank. Another short loop can be made by heading west to Sliderock Lake and then climbing back to the plateau on the west side of the snowbank.

While exploring the basin, watch the weather. It's way too easy—and dangerous—to get caught on the plateau by one of the severe thunderstorms that often roll through here in the afternoon.

Fishing

Three of the Hellroaring Lakes are fishless, and please leave them that way. If you're prepared for mosquitoes, the lower lakes are the perfect place to take your children for their first mountain-lake fishing trip. Each small lake has its own personality, and most support brook trout and cutthroat trout. The trees here provide cover from the wind and a visual break from the rocky terrain above.

When you're tired of catching the numerous smaller trout in the lower lakes, head up the drainage. Hairpin Lake has

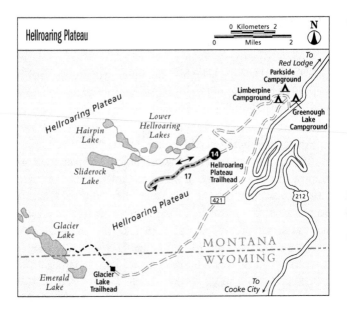

nice cutts, some of which could break a line. On the way back out, make the side trip to Sliderock Lake for some of the healthiest brook trout anywhere in the Beartooths.

15 Glacier Lake

A steep but short day trip to a high-elevation lake basin.

Start: Glacier Lake Trailhead
Distance: 4.0 miles, plus side trips; out-and-back

Maps: USGS Beartooth Butte and Silver Run Peak; RMS Alpine–Mount Maurice; and at least one wilderness-wide map

Finding the trailhead: Drive south from Red Lodge on US 212 for 10.9 miles. Watch for a well-marked turnoff on the right (west) to three Forest Service campgrounds. Stay on this paved road for 0.9 mile until you cross a bridge near the entrance to Limberpine Campground. Immediately after the bridge, the pavement ends and you reach a fork in the road. For Glacier Lake, turn left (southwest). It's a long, slow, bumpy 8 miles to the trailhead, but there's no chance of making a wrong turn because there are no forks or spur roads. The Forest Service has recently improved this road, so you can make it to the trailhead in any vehicle, but you might want an all-wheel drive for the last half mile. Snow usually blocks this gravel road until at least early July. The small parking area is frequently full, so be careful not to take more than one space. There's a toilet and a National Weather Service precipitation gauge on-site. There are undeveloped camping areas and one developed campground along the road on the way up, with three developed campgrounds at the start of the road to Glacier Lake. GPS: 45.00343N / 109.51465W

The Hike

The Glacier Lake area seems nicely suited to a long day of exploring, fishing, photography, and simply enjoying high-elevation majestic vistas. It's easily accessible by a 2-mile trail.

The Forest Service has restricted stock use on this trail due to hazardous conditions for horses.

The trail to Glacier Lake is short but very steep. The trailhead is at 8,680 feet and the lake is at 9,702 feet, but the route actually climbs more than the difference (1,022 feet) in the 2 miles to Glacier Lake. That's because there's a ridge in the middle that's about 800 feet higher than the lake.

After climbing for about half mile, the trail crosses a bridge over Moon Creek. After Moon Creek, the trail gets even steeper—and the higher it goes, the better the scenery.

Shortly after Moon Creek, a faint, unofficial trail veers off to the north to Moon Lake and Shelf Lake. Turn left (west) to stay on what is obviously the main trail. For most of the way, the trail is rough and rock-studded, but it remains easy to follow and without hazards.

Once atop the ridge, you cross some rock shelves on your way down to massive Glacier Lake. Even though the lake sits at 9,702 feet (above timberline), some large trees stand along the shoreline.

The trail reaches the lake at a small dam built long ago to increase the depth of Glacier Lake. A faint trail heads off to the right and goes about halfway around the lake. After a large point jutting out into the water, the trail degenerates into a series of boulder fields and talus slopes. Watch for the amazing number of pikas that inhabit the area.

Bearing right along the north shore of the lake affords views of Triangle Lake and access to Mountain Sheep Lake and Mountain Goat Lake at the head of the basin. Bearing left and across the dam around the south shore of the lake leads directly to Little Glacier Lake, a small jewel just barely separated from Glacier Lake. Continuing south on this trail over a small ridge treats wanderers to the sight of lovely

Emerald Lake. Early in the season, you might have to get your feet wet wading the outlet stream of Glacier Lake to get to Emerald Lake.

Because of topography, Glacier Lake tends to become remarkably windy during midday, so try to arrive early to catch the scenery before the winds start ripping through this valley. Emerald Lake is not quite as windy.

Fishing

It's important to keep track of which state you're in to make sure you have the right fishing license. The state line goes right through Glacier Lake. Little Glacier and Emerald Lakes are in Wyoming.

The ice-cold, swift-running water and high canyon walls make Rock Creek extremely attractive to look at, but these conditions also make life hard for fish. Rock Creek is home to small populations of cutthroat and brook trout. Fish concentrate in the slower water, so look for good holding places out of the current. The main fork of Rock Creek winds in and out of Wyoming and Montana.

Glacier Lake supports cutthroat and brook trout, both of which grow to above-average size. The fish tend to school, with cutthroats working rocky shorelines, so anglers should work the shoreline as well. When water levels are high, water flows between Glacier and Little Glacier Lakes, so the fishery is the same in both. But the fish are easier to find in Little Glacier Lake. Emerald Lake supports both cutts and brookies as well, though they are slightly smaller than those in Glacier.

Cutts are stocked in Mountain Goat Lake and work their way down to Mountain Sheep Lake. Count on more fish in the upper lake and larger ones in the lower.

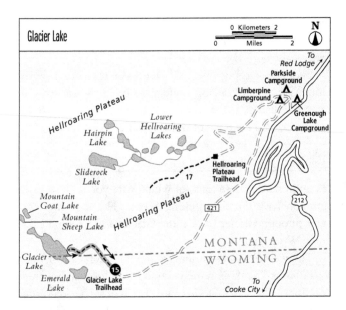

Miles and Directions

0.0 Start at Glacier Lake Trailhead.

0.5 Bridge over Moon Creek.

4.0 Arrive back at Glacier Lake Trailhead.

16 Gardner Lake

A short but steep day trip to a high-elevation lake within sight of the Beartooth Highway.

Start: Gardner Lake Trailhead
Distance: 1.5 miles
out-and-back

Maps: USGS Deep Lake; RMS
Wyoming Beartooths; and at least
one wilderness-wide map

Finding the trailhead: Drive 34.1 miles east from Cooke City or 27.4 miles west from Red Lodge and turn into a large pullout on the south side of the Beartooth Highway (US 212). Plenty of parking; no toilet. GPS: 45.97285N / 109.45195W

The Hike

When you start hiking from a trailhead at 10,595 feet (highest in the Beartooths), there's only one way to go, and the trail to Gardner Lake does exactly that. It's only 0.75 mile to the lake, but it's all steeply downhill to reach it. And, of course, it's a major calf-stretcher to get back to your vehicle.

The trail to Gardner Lake is also the beginning of the Beartooth Loop National Recreation Trail, a long backpacking route.

Gardner Lake is a fairly large lake, and the steep climb down drops to 9,950 feet at the lake, making it a very steep climb to get back to the trailhead from the lake. This extra-high elevation stifles tree growth, so the entire route goes through open, alpine terrain. Along the trail you can note many species of delicate alpine wildflowers, usually downsized by the extreme climate in which they grow.

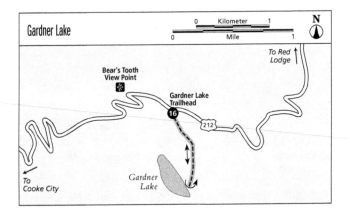

Fishing

Gardner Lake has a good population of easy-to-catch brookies.

Miles and Directions

- **0.0** Start at Gardner Lake Trailhead.
- **0.75** Gardner Lake.
- **1.5** Arrive back at Gardner Lake Trailhead.

17 Hauser Lake

A very easy day trip to a spectacular area close to the highway but still a remote wilderness.

Start: Hauser Lake Trailhead
Distance: 1.5 miles; out-and-back or easy base camp

Maps: USGS Deep Lake; RMS Wyoming Beartooths; and at least one wilderness-wide map

Finding the trailhead: Drive 27.3 miles east from Cooke City or 34.2 miles west from Red Lodge and turn into a large pullout on the north side of the Beartooth Highway (US 212) just east of Long Lake. There's room for five to ten vehicles at the pullout. No toilet. The Forest Service has recently developed a small parking area for the Morrison Jeep Trail with a toilet just south of Long Lake. Take a short gravel road to the parking area. You can start the hike from here or the pullout along the highway. GPS: 44.946113N / 109.495807W

The Hike

This is similar to the Gardner Lake hike without the big hill.

The trail is not well defined in the meadow along the road, so keep your eyes peeled for a few big cairns marking the presence of the trail. Once you get near the trees, the trail becomes easy to follow and stays that way all the way to Hauser Lake. The elevation on this hike is much lower than the trail to Gardner Lake—starting at 9,841 feet and going to the lake at 9,650 feet, and the entire area is mostly open—and very scenic.

If you have some extra time and energy (and don't mind off-trail hiking), you can visit three more lakes with very

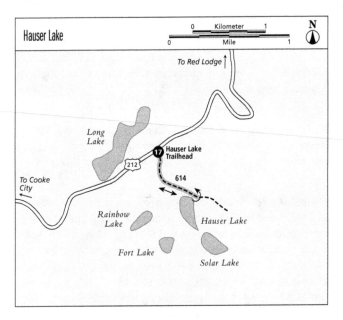

short walks from Hauser Lake: Solar, Fort, and Rainbow Lakes.

Fishing

All four lakes in the vicinity offer fair fishing. Hauser, Solar, and Rainbow Lakes have cutthroats, and Fort has brookies.

Miles and Directions

0.0   Start at Hauser Lake Trailhead.

0.75   Long Lake.

1.5   Arrive back at Hauser Lake Trailhead.

18 Night Lake

A short, flat hike along scenic lakeshores.

Start: Island Lake Trailhead
Distance: 2.0 miles
out-and-back

Maps: USGS, Beartooth Butte;
RMS, Wyoming Beartooths; and
at least one wilderness-wide map

Finding the trailhead: Drive 25.8 miles east from Cooke City or
35.7 miles west from Red Lodge on US 212 and turn north onto a
short access road to the Island Lake Campground. Just before entering the campground, turn right to find the trailhead parking lot. Large
parking area with toilet. Drinking water available near the boat ramp.
GPS: 44.943190N / 109.538964W

The Hike

The trail is about as flat as it gets, but it's still one of the most
scenic routes in the Beartooths. Depending on the time of
year, you might have to get your socks wet crossing Little
Bear Creek right at the trailhead. Later in the season, however, you can usually hop across the stream on exposed rocks.

From the trailhead the trail closely follows the west shore
of Island Lake for most of the first mile. Then it leads less
than a quarter mile over to Night Lake and once again follows the west shore. Night Lake resembles Island Lake, and
the trail again closely follows the shoreline.

Small children love this section of trail, but they tend to
go slowly because there are so many discoveries for them to
make.

This hike gives you lots of options. You can continue
past Night Lake to Flake Lake and even farther to Becker

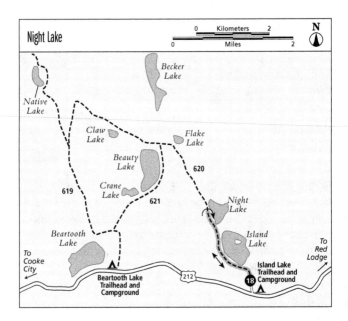

Lake. The way to Becker Lake is well defined, but it's not an official trail, nor does it show up on the Forest Service or USGS maps.

Fishing

Much of this area is easily accessible to horsemen, and as a result, many of the lakes were planted with brook trout in the first half of the twentieth century. The rationale was that brookies are hearty, easily reproduce, and could establish reproducing populations—which they did. Today, brookies provide excellent fishing. However, brookies tend to over-populate these lakes, resulting in smaller fish. On the positive side, 8- to 9-inch brookies may be the tastiest trout of the Beartooths.

Island and Night Lakes have been stocked with rainbows, but now these two lakes are primarily brook trout fisheries. Becker Lake may hold some cutthroats that have migrated down from Albino Lake.

Miles and Directions

0.0   Start at Island Lake Trailhead.

1.0   Night Lake.

2.0   Arrive back at Island Lake Trailhead.

19 Beartooth High Lakes

A truly spectacular route through the famous high lake country of the Beartooths.

Start: Island Lake Trailhead
Distance: 5.9-mile shuttle

Maps: USGS Beartooth Butte; RMS Wyoming Beartooths; and at least one wilderness-wide map

Finding the trailhead: Drive 25.8 miles east from Cooke City or 35.7 miles west from Red Lodge on US 212 and turn north onto a short access road to the Island Lake Campground. Just before entering the campground, turn right to find the trailhead parking lot. Large parking area with toilet. Drinking water available near the boat ramp. GPS: 44.943190N / 109.538964W

To reach the Beartooth Lake Trailhead, drive 22.7 miles east from Cooke City or 38.8 miles west from Red Lodge on US 212 and turn north onto a well-marked turnoff for Beartooth Lake Campground. The trailhead is at the north end of the campground, and the last 100 yards are on a narrow dirt road. Limited parking, so be sure to take only one space. Toilets in the campground. GPS: 44.94648N / 109.58554W

The Hike

This trail is longer than most hikes in this book are, but it's an easy, mostly flat stroll with truly outstanding scenery.

This is one of those shuttle trails that require arranging transportation in advance. Leave a vehicle or bicycle at the Beartooth Lake Trailhead, or arrange with another party to start at Beartooth Lake and meet along the trail for lunch so you can trade keys. The trail can be hiked from either direction with no extra difficulty, but this description starts at the Island Lake Trailhead.

Plan on taking the entire day to cover the distance, leaving plenty of time to enjoy the scenery. Carry a water filter to save weight rather than packing in several full water bottles; the route follows streams and lakes virtually every step of the way.

You might have to get your socks wet right after the trailhead where the trail crosses Little Bear Creek, which flows from Island Lake to Beartooth Lake. In August and September you might be able to walk across on rocks, but usually not in July.

After going along Island, Night, and Flake Lakes, the trail turns west just after Flake Lake and soon drops down to Beauty Lake, where the scenery justifies the name. Just before the lake, look for Trail 621 heading off to the south along the east shore of Beauty Lake. Turn left (south) at this junction.

For about a mile, the trail follows the east shoreline of Beauty Lake. Shortly after leaving Beauty Lake, the trail goes by Crane Lake. It's worth the 100-yard side trip to relax by this scenic lake with a sandy shoreline.

From Crane Lake, it's a gradual downhill walk through mostly forested terrain to Beartooth Lake. You cross Little Bear Creek again just before reaching the trailhead. Instead of crossing where the trail hits the creek, follow a path to your left along the creek for about 50 yards, where you might find a footbridge.

Fishing

Fishing along this trail leans toward brook trout, although several other species have been planted over the brook trout populations. Fishing is usually excellent in lakes with

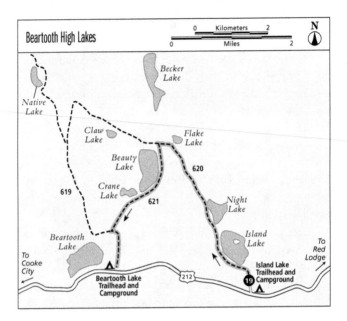

brookies, but some days even these fish are hard to catch—
and sometimes hardware users will outfish the fly fishermen.

Beauty Lake has had cutts stocked over the brookies.
Claw, Horseshoe, and Beartooth Lakes have all had lake trout
planted to feed on the brookies to control their population.
Beartooth Lake has had several other species introduced,
including rainbows, cutts, goldens, and grayling.

Miles and Directions

0.0 Start at Island Lake Trailhead.

1.0 Night Lake.

2.5 Flake Lake.

3.2 Junction with Trail 621 to Beartooth Lake Trailhead; turn left.

3.3 Upper end of Beauty Lake.

4.3 Lower end of Beauty Lake.

4.5 Junction with trail to Crane Lake: turn left.

5.9 Arrive at Beartooth Lake Trailhead.

20 Becker Lake

An easy hike with a remarkable number of lakes to enjoy along the way.

Start: Island Lake Trailhead
Distance: 7.0 miles out-and-back

Maps: USGS Beartooth Butte; RMS Wyoming Beartooths; and at least one wilderness-wide map

Finding the trailhead: Drive 25.8 miles east from Cooke City or 35.7 miles west from Red Lodge on US 212 and turn north onto a short access road to the Island Lake Campground. Just before entering the campground, turn right to find the trailhead parking lot. Large parking area with toilet. Drinking water available near the boat ramp. GPS: 44.943190N / 109.538964W

The Hike

This is a great day hike for families and children. Expect to get your feet wet, though, because three safe stream crossings have no bridges. The trail gains only 175 feet in elevation over 3.5 miles, but just because it's flat doesn't mean it's lacking in scenery. To the contrary, this is one of the most scenic routes in the Beartooths.

From the trailhead the trail crosses an inlet stream before reaching the boat ramp parking area, then crosses another stream. From here the trail closely follows the west shore of Island Lake for most of the first mile, then leads less than a quarter mile to Night Lake, once again following the west shore. Small children love this section of trail, but they tend to go slowly because there are so many discoveries for them to make.

Continue past Flake Lake, also to the east, until you leave Trail 620 and head straight north (to the right) toward Becker Lake. Be alert not to miss the trail heading to Becker Lake—this is not an official Forest Service trail, nor does it show up on the Forest Service or USGS maps. This "unofficial" trail is, however, as well-defined as and more heavily used than most official trails.

The trail turns north in a wet meadow just after you leave Flake Lake behind and Trail 620 turns to the west. The first 50 feet or so is overgrown and hard to see. Then it becomes an excellent trail and almost as crowded as Trail 620. If you miss the trail, simply head cross-country along the continuous lake between Flake Lake and Jeff Lake. Stay on the west side of the lakes, and you'll soon see the trail.

Go between Mutt Lake and Jeff Lake, crossing over a small stream between the lakes. The two lakes are essentially one lake, since the elevation drop between them is about 5 inches. Just past Mutt and Jeff, navigate through a small boulder field. The trail disappears here, so look ahead to where it's clearly defined.

After climbing a small hill (the only one on this trip), hikers are treated to their first view of Becker Lake, with incredibly sheer cliffs on its west bank and 11,409-foot Lonesome Mountain dominating the northern horizon.

Fishing

This hike has become popular with anglers, in part because there is very little elevation gain. The fishing along this route leans toward brook trout, a good fish for youngsters learning to fish as well as oldsters looking for lots of action. Keep in mind that brook trout are often easier to catch on hardware (lures) than hackle (flies). Island and Night Lakes have been

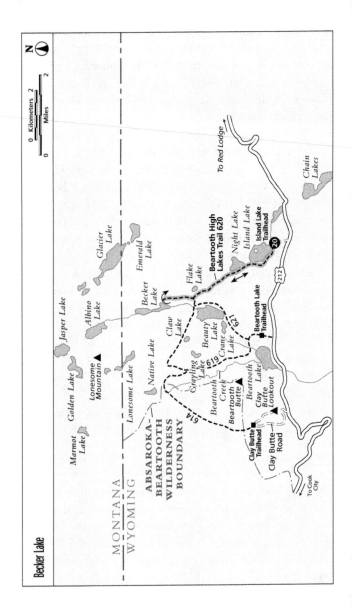

Becker Lake

stocked with rainbows, but now these two lakes are primarily brook trout fisheries. Becker Lake may hold some cutthroats that have migrated down from Albino Lake.

For some variety and a chance to hook cutthroat trout, head up over the saddle at the end of Becker Lake into Montana and to Albino Lake, which is stocked on a four-year cycle and also has some natural reproduction to provide some variation in size.

Golden and Jasper Lakes, just over the hill from Albino, harbor slightly larger cutts. Heading west cross-country, anglers can try the Cloverleaf Lakes, which sport some of the best cutthroat fishing in the Beartooths.

Miles and Directions

0.0 Start at Island Lake Trailhead.

1.0 Night Lake.

2.5 Flake Lake.

2.7 Turn off Beartooth High Lakes Trail 620.

3.2 Mutt and Jeff Lakes.

3.5 Becker Lake.

7.0 Arrive back at Island Lake Trailhead.

21 Beauty Lake

A nice day hike suitable for children and families.

Start: Beartooth Lake Trailhead	**Maps:** USGS Beartooth Butte;
Distance: 4.8 miles	RMS Wyoming Beartooths; and at
out-and-back	least one wilderness-wide map

Finding the trailhead: Drive 22.7 miles east from Cooke City or 38.8 miles west from Red Lodge and turn north on a well-marked turnoff for Beartooth Lake Campground. Once in the campground, it might take a few minutes to find the trailhead. A likely looking spot on the left just past the entrance is actually a picnic area and boat launch. The trailhead is at the north end of the campground. The last 100 yards to the trailhead is a narrow dirt road. Limited parking, so be sure to take only one space; toilets; camping in the campground at the trailhead. GPS: 44.94648N / 109.58554W

The Hike

This trail leaves from a major vehicle campground and is one of the most accessible trails in the Beartooths. Consequently, the trail to Beauty Lake receives heavy use compared to most other trails in the Beartooths, but not heavy compared to short day hikes in most national parks.

After crossing Little Bear Creek on a footbridge by the trailhead, hike along the stream for about 100 yards until you see the trail heading off to the right through a meadow. The trail can get faint here, but it becomes well defined on the other side of the meadow and stays that way all the way to Beauty Lake.

In less than a quarter mile after the trailhead, the trail splits. Trail 619 veers off to the left toward Beartooth Butte. Go right on Trail 621 to Beauty Lake.

A gradual climb of about 500 feet leads through lush forest with lots of wildflowers and mushrooms. The trail is rocky in a few places but is still nicely suited for families with small children. It's rare for such great scenery to grace such a short hike. The trail climbs gradually to Beauty Lake, but it's all downhill on the way back to the trailhead.

At 1.4 miles look for Crane Lake off to the left (west) and a spur trail splitting off toward the lake. Crane Lake might not be your destination, but it's nice enough to be. The lake has a sandy shoreline, rare in the Beartooths.

After checking out Crane Lake, return to the main trail and continue north for less than quarter mile to Beauty Lake. All visitors probably agree that this lake lives up to its name. This large, clear, alpine lake boasts several sandy beaches just right for wading on a warm day.

Fishing

Beartooth Lake has been stocked with lake trout, which have thinned the brook trout population. The remaining brookies are larger than average size. Beartooth Lake has had several introductions of other species including rainbows, cutts, goldens, and grayling.

Even though other species have been planted in Beauty Lake, the fishing is still dominated by brook trout. Crane Lake has had cutts stocked over the brookies. Fishing in both lakes is excellent.

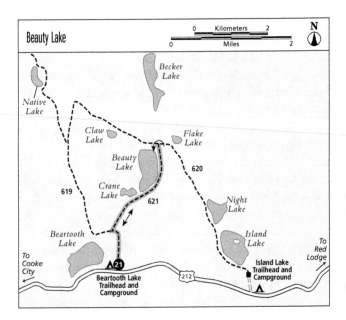

Miles and Directions

- **0.0** Start at Beartooth Lake Trailhead.
- **0.2** Junction with trail to Beauty Lake; turn right.
- **1.4** Junction with trail to Crane Lake; turn right.
- **1.6** South edge of Beauty Lake.
- **2.4** Junction with Beartooth High Lakes Trail 620.
- **4.8** Arrive back at Beartooth Lake Trailhead.

22 Native Lake

A beautiful and accessible lake with an incredible number of alpine lakes within easy walking distance.

Start: Beartooth Lake Trailhead
Distance: 8.0 miles, not counting side trips; out-and-back with shuttle option
Maps: USGS Beartooth Butte, Muddy Creek, Castle Mountain

and Silver Run Peak; RMS Wyoming Beartooths and Alpine–Mount Maurice; and at least one wilderness-wide map

Finding the trailhead: Drive 22.7 miles east from Cooke City or 38.8 miles west from Red Lodge and turn north on a well-marked turnoff for Beartooth Lake Campground. Once in the campground, it might take a few minutes to find the trailhead. A likely looking spot on the left just past the entrance is actually a picnic area and boat launch. The trailhead is at the north end of the campground. The last 100 yards to the trailhead is a narrow dirt road. Limited parking, so be sure to take only one space; toilets; camping in the campground at the trailhead. GPS: 44.94648N / 109.58554W

The Hike

How to get to Native Lake can be a tough decision. Going in at the Beartooth Lake Trailhead, as described in this book, is the shortest way. But the Clay Butte and Island Lake Trailheads also offer access to this area.

Regardless of which trailhead you use, the way into Native Lake can be nearly effortless compared to many trails in the Beartooths. All three trails go through gorgeous, open, alpine country, dotted with lakes and carpeted with wildflowers.

After crossing Little Bear Creek on a footbridge by the trailhead, hike along the stream for about 100 yards until you see the trail heading off to the right through a meadow. Less than a quarter mile from the trailhead, watch for the junction with Trail 621 to Beauty Lake. Turn left to stay on Trail 619, and head for Beartooth Butte.

Start out hiking around the north edge of Beartooth Lake on the edge of some moist meadows. Beartooth Butte provides a magnificent backdrop on the western horizon most of the way into Native Lake. The trail crosses Beartooth Creek twice, but it's usually easy to find a way across on rocks without getting your feet wet.

At the junction with Beartooth High Lakes Trail 620, bear left and keep going north on Trail 619. About a half mile after the junction, watch for a trail and a string of cairns going off to the west through the pass on the north side of Beartooth Butte. These cairns lead down to Trail 614 to Clay Butte Trailhead.

Continue northwest on the main trail another half mile to Native Lake. The trail is well defined the entire way.

From Native Lake, there are plenty of options for adventurous side trips. This is a great place to practice using a compass and topo map.

As an option, you can arrange a shuttle at a different trailhead to avoid retracing your steps on the way out. With two vehicles, it's best to leave a vehicle at Beartooth Lake (8,900 feet elevation) and go in at the Clay Butte Trailhead (9,600 feet elevation).

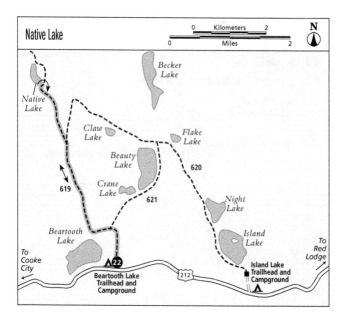

Native Lake

Fishing

Native Lake is a cutthroat exception to the brook trout theme found throughout this area. If the cutts are being stubborn, many of the lakes in the area sport voracious populations of brookies. The nearby Beartooth High Lakes Trail provides access to many of these, with lake trout having been added to both T and Lamb Lakes.

Miles and Directions

0.0   Start at Beartooth Lake Trailhead.

0.2   Junction with Trail 621 to Beauty Lake; turn left.

2.9 Junction with Beartooth High Lakes Trail 620; turn left.

3.6 Turnoff to Trail 614 and Clay Butte Trailhead; turn right.

4.0 Native Lake.

8.0 Arrive back at Beartooth Lake Trailhead.

23 Crazy Creek Falls

A very short uphill trek along a magnificent cascade of white water.

Start: Crazy Creek Trailhead
Distance: 1.0 mile out-and-back

Maps: USGS Jim Smith Peak; RMS Wyoming Beartooths; and at least one wilderness-wide map

Finding the trailhead: Drive 11 miles east from Cooke City or 50.5 miles west from Red Lodge and turn north into a turnout across the highway from the Crazy Creek Campground. Limited parking; no toilet; vehicle campground with toilets across the highway. GPS: 44.94292N / 109.77359W

The Hike

The centerpiece of the area, Crazy Creek Falls is only a short walk from the trailhead. Even if you don't take a longer foray up Crazy Creek, do stop for a few minutes to savor the raw beauty of Crazy Creek Falls.

You can hear the falls right from the trailhead, and after walking up the trail about 100 feet, you can see this massive cascade. The trail continues along the falls for about a half mile with several great viewpoints of the falls. If you stop to see Crazy Creek Falls in June, you'll be amazed at how much water is tumbling out of the mountains.

Miles and Directions

0.0 Start at Crazy Creek Trailhead.

0.5 Crazy Creek Falls.

1.0 Arrive back at Crazy Creek Trailhead.

24 Kersey Lake

A short, flat trail to a large, forested lake.

Start: Clarks Fork Trailhead
Distance: 3.0 miles
out-and-back

Maps: USGS Pyramid Mountain;
RMS Alpine–Mount Maurice; and
at least one wilderness-wide map

Finding the trailhead: Drive 3.4 miles east from Cooke City or
58.1 miles west from Red Lodge and turn north onto Forest Road
306. Drive about a half mile to the trailhead. Be careful not to go to
the special trailhead for backcountry horsemen, which is just west
of the hiker trailhead. There's a huge trailhead with plenty of parking,
a toilet, picnic area, and interpretive displays. GPS: 45.01762N /
109.86935W

The Hike

To find Kersey Lake, take Trail 3 from the Clarks Fork Trailhead. Immediately after leaving the trailhead, you cross an
awe-inspiring wooden footbridge over the Clarks Fork of
the Yellowstone where it gushes through a narrow gorge.

The first mile of the trail is split—the east path is for
hikers and the west for horses. After about a half mile, turn
right (east) at the well-marked junction with the Kersey Lake
jeep road.

From this point, it's about another mile to the east shore
of massive Kersey Lake. Just before you reach the lake, the
trail to Lake Vernon veers off to the right (east).

There are cabins with vehicle access to the south shore of
the lake. These are inholdings; one is a Forest Service rental

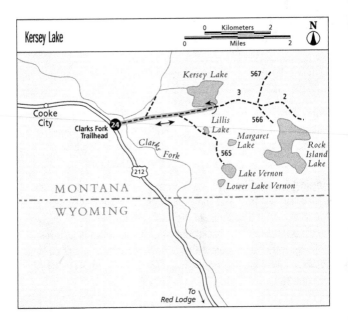

cabin. Kersey Lake is not within the Absaroka-Beartooth Wilderness.

Miles and Directions

- **0.0** Start at Clarks Fork Trailhead.
- **0.5** Junction with Kersey Lake jeep road; turn right.
- **1.2** Junction with Lake Vernon Trail 565; turn left.
- **1.5** East shore of Kersey Lake.
- **3.0** Arrive back at Clarks Fork Trailhead.

25 Lake Vernon

An easy day hike to two forested lakes.

Start: Clarks Fork Trailhead
Distance: 5.0 miles
out-and-back

Maps: USGS Fossil Lake; RMS
Cooke City–Cutoff Mountain; and
at least one wilderness-wide map

Finding the trailhead: Drive 3.4 miles east from Cooke City or
58.1 miles west from Red Lodge and turn north onto Forest Road
306. Drive about a half mile to the trailhead. Be careful not to go to
the special trailhead for backcountry horsemen, which is just west of
the hiker trailhead. A huge trailhead with plenty of parking, toilet, picnic area, and interpretive displays. GPS: 45.01762N / 109.86935W

The Hike

Lake Vernon is a great choice for a day hike with small children. The trail is well maintained and easy to follow all the
way as it passes through a rich, unburned forest. Keep a sharp
eye out for moose, especially in the big meadow just before
Lillis Lake.

The trail doesn't have abundant drinking water, so bring
an extra bottle. Like all trails in this area, mosquitoes can be
bothersome, especially early in the summer.

To reach Lake Vernon, take Trail 3 from the Clarks Fork
Trailhead for about 1.2 miles to a well-signed junction with
Trail 565 to Lake Vernon. Turn right (south) and head up a
moderate grade. After another half mile or so, look for little,
jewel-like Lillis Lake in the foreground with majestic Pilot
Peak and Index Peak as a backdrop.

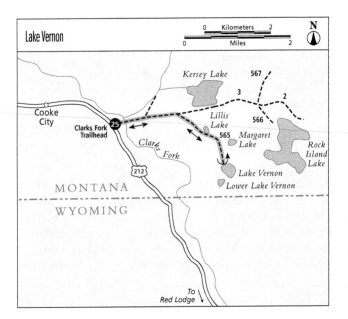

The trail continues around the northwest shoreline of Lillis Lake less than a mile more to the destination, Lake Vernon. This forest-lined lake is larger than Lillis but offers a similar view of Pilot and Index. Just south of Lake Vernon is Lower Lake Vernon, more appropriately called Reed Lake on some maps because it's little more than a scenic marsh.

On the way out of Lake Vernon, the trail climbs the biggest hill of the trip, about a half mile long. Once at the top, however, it's downhill all the way to the trailhead.

Fishing

This short day hike offers some surprising fishing. Brook trout have trouble reproducing in Lillis Lake, and the smaller population translates into bigger brookies. Be sure to stop at this small lake on the way to Vernon, which hosts both cutthroat and brook trout. Just over the hill, you could find yourself alone catching stocked cutthroats at Margaret Lake.

Miles and Directions

0.0 Start at Clarks Fork Trailhead.

0.5 Junction with Kersey Lake jeep road; turn right.

1.2 Junction with Lake Vernon Trail 565; turn right.

1.8 Lillis Lake.

2.5 Lake Vernon.

5.0 Arrive back at Clarks Fork Trailhead.

26 Rock Island Lake

An easy day hike to an unusually large, sprawling, forest-lined lake.

Start: Clarks Fork Trailhead
Distance: 6.0 miles out-and-back

Maps: USGS Fossil Lake; RMS Cooke City–Cutoff Mountain; and at least one wilderness-wide map

Finding the trailhead: Drive 3.4 miles east from Cooke City or 58.1 miles west from Red Lodge and turn north onto Forest Road 306. Drive about a half mile to the trailhead. Be careful not to go to the special trailhead for backcountry horsemen, which is just west of the hiker trailhead. A huge trailhead with plenty of parking, toilet, picnic area, and interpretive displays. GPS: 45.01762N / 109.86935W

The Hike

Rock Island Lake is different from many high-elevation lakes. Instead of forming a small, concise oval in the end of a cirque, it sprawls across flat and forested terrain, seemingly branching off in every direction. Visitors can spend an entire day just walking around it.

To get to Rock Island Lake, take Trail 3 from the Clarks Fork Trailhead to the junction with Trail 566 to Rock Island Lake. Turn right (east) here for about another half mile to the lake. The trail is well used and well maintained the entire way with only one hill (near Kersey Lake). The 1988 fires scorched the area around Kersey Lake but missed Rock Island Lake.

Because Rock Island Lake is so easy to reach (3 miles on a near-level trail), it's a perfect choice for a family planning their first trip into the Absaroka-Beartooth Wilderness. Drinking water is readily available on the trail and at the lake (it must be boiled or filtered), but the mosquitoes are bad in early summer.

Fishing

This popular lake has a combination of homegrown brookies and cutthroats stocked on a three-year rotation, both of which grow well in this lake. The fishing should generally be good enough to count on for dinner.

Miles and Directions

0.0 Start at Clarks Fork Trailhead.

0.5 Junction with Kersey Lake Jeep Road; turn right.

1.2 Junction with Trail 565 to Lake Vernon; turn left.

1.5 Kersey Lake.

2.4 Junction with Trail 566 to Rock Island Lake; turn right.

3.0 Rock Island Lake.

6.0 Arrive back at Clarks Fork Trailhead.

27 Lady of the Lake

An easy day hike to a gorgeous, forested lake.

Start: Lady of the Lake Trailhead
Distance: 3.6 miles
out-and-back

Maps: USGS Cooke City; RMS
Cooke City–Cutoff Mountain; and
at least one wildernesswide map

Finding the trailhead: Drive 2 miles east from Cooke City or 59.5
miles west from Red Lodge on US 212 and turn north onto the Lulu
Pass Road, less than a quarter mile west of Colter Campground. Drive
about 1.5 miles to the Forest Service trailhead on your right (east)
of the Lulu Pass Road just before you cross Fisher Creek and before
you reach the Goose Lake Jeep Road. You can also access Lady of
the Lake from an old unofficial trailhead about a half mile farther up
the road. No toilet. Undeveloped camping sites at the trailhead and
nearby. GPS: 45.04609N / 109.91201W

The Hike

Lady of the Lake is an ideal choice for an easy day hike
with small children. Besides being a short hike, watching the
weather isn't as critical as it is at the higher elevations.

It's about 0.3 mile from the new official trailhead to the
old unofficial trailhead. After crossing Fisher Creek on a
bridge, the trail goes by a small inholding with a cabin and
then heads down a well-maintained, forestlined trail to Lady
of the Lake. The trail sign says "1 mile" to the lake, but it's
probably more like 1.5 miles. The trail breaks out of the trees
into a large marshy meadow at the foot of the lake. The trail
goes up and down, but there are no big hills.

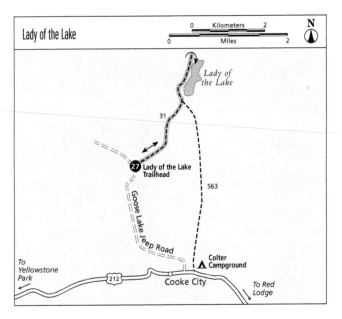

Just before the lake, Trail 563 heads off to the right (south) to Lower Lady of the Lake Trailhead near Colter Campground on US 212. (Trail 563 also offers fairly easy access to Lady of the Lake, but the route described here is much shorter and faster.) Stay to the left on Trail 31 to the lake.

The return trip involves more climbing than the way in, so allow extra time, especially if traveling with small children.

Fishing

Lady of the Lake is a personal favorite of places to take kids for their first wilderness camping experience. The hike is easy, and the brook trout are always willing. For those with some wilderness experience, there are four small lakes nestled in the trees to the southeast. They're a bit tough to find, but they promise solitude. Grayling are stocked in Mosquito Lake when available, while the other lakes are scheduled for stocking with cutthroats. Don't bother to fish Fisher Creek. Acid effluent from mines abandoned before environmental protection laws were in place keeps this stream close to sterile.

Miles and Directions

- **0.0** Start at Lady of the Lake Trailhead.
- **0.3** Old access point and trailhead.
- **1.3** Junction with Trail 563; stay left.
- **1.8** Lady of the Lake.
- **3.6** Arrive back at Lady of the Lake Trailhead.

28 Passage Falls

An easy day hike to a gorgeous waterfall.

Start: Passage Falls Trailhead
Distance: 4.0 miles
out-and-back

Maps: USGS The Pyramid; RMS
Gardiner–Mount Wallace; and at
least one wilderness-wide map

Finding the trailhead: Drive south from Livingston on US 89 for 16 miles and turn left (east) at a well-marked turn onto the Mill Creek Road. You cross the Yellowstone River after half mile. Continue driving southeast on Mill Creek Road (FR 486), which turns to gravel after 5.6 miles. (You can cut about 2 miles off the route by taking the East River Road south from Livingston and turning left on the well-signed Mill Creek Road.) For the Passage Falls Trailhead, continue 4 miles past the West Fork Road or 2.7 miles past Snowbank Campground. A large trailhead with a one-way road through it and ample parking, including room for horse trailers; no toilet. GPS: 45.49752N / 110.51965W

The Hike

The trail is double-wide except for the last 0.2 mile, where you turn left onto a single track for a small drop down to the waterfall. This last section has a few steep spots, so hang on to the kids. The route follows the stream until the junction. It's quite heavily traveled, so don't expect to be alone. The trail goes right down to the falls for an up-close and personal view.

The waterfall is on Gallatin National Forest land but right on the edge of an inholding that's being developed

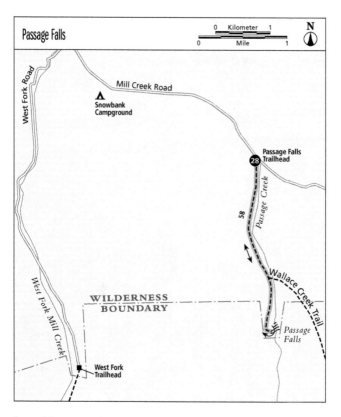

Passage Falls

0   Kilometer   1

0   Mile   1

N

West Fork Road

Mill Creek Road

Snowbank Campground

Passage Falls Trailhead

28

58

Passage Creek

Wallace Creek Trail

WILDERNESS BOUNDARY

West Fork Mill Creek

Passage Falls

West Fork Trailhead

for wilderness cabin sites. Be sure to respect the landowners' rights and stay on the trail.

Unfortunately, this trail is open to motorized vehicles, so you might see a dirt bike or ATV on the trail.

Miles and Directions

0.0   Start at Passage Falls Trailhead.

1.2   Junction with Wallace Creek Trail; turn right.

1.8 Boundary of private property.

2.0 Passage Falls.

4.0 Arrive back at Passage Falls Trailhead.

29 Pine Creek Falls

A moderate day hike to a beautiful mountain waterfall.

Start: Pine Creek Trailhead
Distance: 2.0 miles
out-and-back

Maps: USGS T USGS Emigrant
and Mt. Cowen; RMS Gardiner-
Mount Wallace; and at least one
wilderness-wide map

Finding the trailhead: Drive south from Livingston on US 89 for
3 miles. Then turn left (east) on East River Road (Highway 540) and
head south for 7.5 miles; 0.7 mile past the cabin community of Pine
Creek, turn left (east) onto paved FR 202. Go to the end of this road
(2.6 miles, paved all the way) where Trail 47 starts at the far end of
the campground. For an alternate route from US 89, take Pine Creek
Road between mile markers 43 and 44. Ample parking; toilet; Forest
Service vehicle campground at trailhead with toilet. GPS: 45.49752N
/ 110.51965W

The Hike

From the trailhead, the first 0.2 mile of Trail 47 is easy and
very well defined. At the junction with the trail to George
Lake, turn left (east). The trail remains deceptively flat for
the next 0.8 mile. At the end of the flat stretch, you stand at
the foot of beautiful Pine Creek Falls. This is far enough for
some hikers who have heard about the next 4 miles. In those
4 miles, the trail climbs more than 3,000 feet up to Pine
Creek Lake, definitely not a Best Easy Day Hike.

The best time to visit Pine Creek Falls is between July
15 and September 30. Before school starts, youth camps use
the trail heavily.

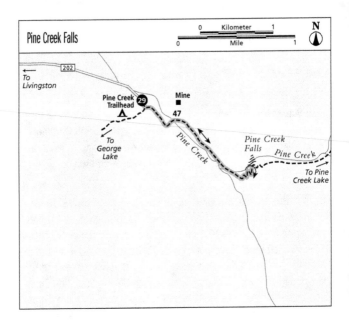

Pine Creek Falls

Miles and Directions

- **0.0** Start at Pine Creek Trailhead.
- **0.2** Junction with George Lake Trail; turn left.
- **1.0** Pine Creek Falls.
- **2.0** Arrive back at Pine Creek Trailhead.

About the Author

Bill Schneider has spent more than fifty years on the hiking trails of Montana. It started during college in 1965 when he worked on a trail crew in Glacier National Park. He spent the 1970s publishing *Montana Outdoors* magazine for the Montana Department of Fish, Wildlife and Parks—and covering as many miles of trails as possible on weekends and holidays.

In 1979 Bill and his partner Mike Sample founded Falcon Publishing, where he worked as publisher for twenty years. Along the way, he wrote twenty-four books and hundreds of magazine and newspaper articles on wildlife, outdoor recreation, and environmental issues.

For twelve years, Bill taught classes on bicycling, backpacking, zero impact camping, and hiking in bear country for the Yellowstone Institute, a nonprofit educational organization in Yellowstone National Park.

In 2000 Bill retired from his position as publisher of Falcon Publishing, which has grown into the premier publisher of outdoor recreation guidebooks with more than 800 titles in print. He spent the next ten years working as an online columnist, outdoor and travel writer, and publishing consultant until finally discovering the true concept of retirement.

He lives in Helena, Montana, works as little as possible, and stays focused on trying to hike, bicycle, and fish himself to death.

Books by Bill Schneider

Where the Grizzly Walks, 1977

Hiking Montana, 1979, last revised 2014

The Dakota Image, 1980

The Yellowstone River, 1985

Best Hikes on the Continental Divide, 1988

The Flight of the Nez Perce, 1988

The Tree Giants, 1988

Hiking the Beartooths, 1995

Bear Aware: A Quick Reference Bear Country Survival Guide, 1996, last revised 2012

Hiking Carlsbad Caverns & Guadalupe Mountains National Parks, 1996, last revised 2005

Hiking Canyonlands and Arches National Parks, 1997, last revised 2014

Best Easy Day Hikes Canyonlands and Arches, 1997, last revised 2014

Best Easy Day Hikes Yellowstone, 1997, last revised 2012

Hiking Yellowstone National Park, 1997, last revised 2012

Backpacking Tips (coauthor), 1998

Best Easy Day Hikes Absaroka-Beartooth Wilderness, 1998, last revised 2015

Best Easy Day Hikes Grand Teton, 1999, last revised 2010

Hiking Grand Teton National Park, 1999, last revised 2010

Best Backpacking Vacations Northern Rockies, 2002

Hiking the Absaroka-Beartooth Wilderness, 1998, last revised 2015

Where the Grizzly Walks, 2003 (complete rewrite)

Bear Country Behavior (a *Backpacker* magazine book), 2012

Hiking Montana Bozeman, 2015

Glacier National Park: Reflections, 2020

THE TEN ESSENTIALS OF HIKING

American Hiking Society

Whether you plan to be gone for a couple of hours or several months, make sure to pack these items. Become familiar with these items and know how to use them.

1. Appropriate Footwear
Happy feet make for pleasant hiking. Think about traction, support, and protection when selecting well-fitting shoes or boots.

2. Navigation
While phones and GPS units are handy, they aren't always reliable in the backcountry; consider carrying a paper map and compass as a backup and know how to use them.

3. Water (and a way to purify it)
As a guideline, plan for half a liter of water per hour in moderate temperatures/terrain. Carry enough water for your trip and know where and how to treat water while you're out on the trail.

4. Food
Pack calorie-dense foods to help fuel your hike, and carry an extra portion in case you are out longer than expected.

5. Rain Gear & Dry-Fast Layers
The weatherman is not always right. Dress in layers to adjust to changing weather and activity levels. Wear moisture-wicking clothes and carry a warm hat.

6. Safety Items (light, fire, and a whistle)
Have means to start an emergency fire, signal for help, and see the trail and your map in the dark.

7. First Aid Kit
Supplies to treat illness or injury are only as helpful as your knowledge of how to use them. Take a class to gain the skills needed to administer first aid and CPR.

8. Knife or Multi-Tool
With countless uses, a multi-tool can help with gear repair and first aid.

9. Sun Protection
Sunscreen, sunglasses, and sun-protective clothing should be used in every season regardless of temperature or cloud cover.

10. Shelter
Protection from the elements in the event you are injured or stranded is necessary. A lightweight, inexpensive space blanket is a great option.

Find other helpful resources at AmericanHiking.org/hiking-resources